Howlett

Before the living God

Before the
Living God

Ruth Burrows

DIMENSION BOOKS
DENVILLE, NEW JERSEY 07834

Published by

DIMENSION BOOKS
Denville, New Jersey

First American Edition   1981
ISBN # 0-87193-155-9

Without beauty, without majesty,
we looked on him—and turned away our eyes.

Is 53:2

CONTENTS

TO MOTHER ELSA OF JESUS
Carmelite

Dear Elsa,

Here I am at last complying with your continual urging to write the story of my life. It is nearly a year since you were here—(O blessed three months)—and suggested this. In the first place you thought that, by doing so, my thoughts would clarify and that I would come to know myself and hence God's way of love with me. You knew as none other, save one, perhaps, the state of darkness and anguish which was my lot. You, as no other, understood it and knew that I too understood it if only I would be true to my inmost heart and its deep intuitions. But you thought also that my experience would help others; that the very complexity of my nature, its tortuous searchings and above all, the gift—a dubious gift I am tempted to say—of self-analysis, have led me to an understanding and insight that could benefit others. As for the first motive, it seems to me I no longer need this exposition for myself, at least not in the sense you first conceived. Already, it seems to me, I have grasped the mystery of my life. One long searching look into my past and I see, there in its depths, the face of Christ gazing back at me.

Had you not urged me to it, Elsa, I would never have presumed that an account of my life might be a help to others but since you have done so I am prepared to consider why it might be useful. My experience with other people, as you know, is not wide. It has been limited to those whose sole aim in life is to love and serve God. For many years I have been in a position privileged to share the intimate

1

thoughts, desires, anxieties and joys of such people. My experience is not wide but deep, for I seem to have the gift of drawing from others the ability to look at and express themselves. I have found that drawing on my own experience has helped them, and I, in my privileged position, have learnt a lot from them.

If I were to say that what I want to show people is that what really matters is utter trust in God; that this trust cannot be there until we have lost all self-trust and are rooted in poverty; that we must be willing to go to God with empty hands, and that the whole meaning of our existence and the one consuming desire of the heart of God is that we should let ourselves be loved, many spiritual persons would smile at my naïveté. They are likely to murmur: 'But we know all that; we can read that in any spiritual book. Does she think she is telling us something new?' All I can say is that, although I too have known this in theory, it is only now that it is integrated into my life. At least so it seems. Probably in five years time or even next year, I will realise that now I know next to nothing about it. What is more, looking at my dear friends, living for God, wanting only him, I see in fact that something is yet wanting to them. They have not come to perfect trust. They feel they are spiritual failures because this has not happened to them and that has not happened to them; they feel they have missed out on something because their experience carries none of the features which treatises on prayer and the contemplative life seem to demand as signs of a truly authentic spiritual life. They know they are loved by God and are pleasing to him and yet there is an indefinable anxiety which inhibits that total surrender to love which bridges the gap between the virtuous man or woman and the saint. It seems to me that God is asking one thing more and only one thing more, and this, precisely, is what they are refusing to give. It is, in fact, the deepest self-denial and so different from the ways in which they are seeking to do things for God and, as it were, trying to wrest God's good pleasure from his reluctant heart. This refusal seems to me to spring from lack of insight and understanding, certainly not from lack of good will. I see these dear people, self-giving, generous to a degree, full of love for God and yet still anxious, still hesitant before the last step which will release them from themselves and bury them in God. I see them turning, with a sense of failure, to

2

new ideas on prayer which might perhaps 'work better' though this is certainly not the term they would use. Yoga, Zen, Pentecostalism—these may have something to offer. I long to convince them that there is no need for this, that here and now, in their present 'unsatisfactory' state, in their 'failure', God is giving himself to them; that this state of poverty is precisely what he wants and his way into them. He has laboured with love to open up this way and will they now block it? I could tell them that, in fact, they are turning from the straight path up the mountain, the path of poverty, and choosing the winding road of spiritual riches.

I have known this doubt, this tearing anxiety to a frightful degree. For nearly thirty years I have groped in darkness. But to some extent, at any rate, now I see. In these days of sharing and dialogue, it cannot be thought out of place, pride and presumption, to want to share my insight with others. There is absolutely nothing extraordinary or 'interesting' in my life. It is completely common-place. But it may be that the sheer commonplaceness will help others. I feel that it is in the story of my life, of my own search and journey, that what I want to say will be revealed and may strike home in a way that a purely theoretical exposition of these truths will never do. Here again, my own experience gives this assurance.

The autobiography of another woman has been, from the early years of my suffering, difficult spiritual life, one of God's ways of bringing me light and peace. I saw my own self reflected in her, and her growth and insight became my insight. I refer to St Thérèse of Lisieux. You know, Elsa, what an inspiration she has been to me. Many a time we have talked together of her. Words cannot express what I understand about Thérèse and her mission. Only in you have I found a similar grasp of her doctrine. I fear that, in great part, her message has fallen on deaf ears. She has not been listened to. And if she has, to some extent, been understood in the past—though I fear I must question how many have really understood her—she is overlooked today. Yet it seems to me there is a crying need that what she has taught us should be given to the modern world. I am told that the modern generation has no time for her. I would answer that they do not know her. I have dealings with young religious, aspirants for the religious life, and young women in the world bent

3

on living for God. When they approach me with their aspirations and problems, I find myself spontaneously speaking of Thérèse. I get them to read passages from her writings. There they find their answer. She is 'dead on'.

Rejecting the idea of an autobiography, I was prepared to write a book on Thérèse but you stuck to your original idea that I should write my life for, you insisted, this would be in itself an exposition of St Thérèse's doctrine, but in the idiom of our times. Yes, I think this may be true; at any rate, I hope it is so. I hope too it will be a little treatise on Carmel and the spiritual inheritance to which I owe so much.

This book will reveal nothing to you, Elsa. It is true there are details of my life which you do not know, but my soul you know. It is a rare thing, I am sure, for a person to feel utterly understood by another, to be completely confident that the other is not dependent on what you tell about yourself but rather is given an intuition which embraces the whole of oneself and one's relation to God. This priceless gift was given to me. It is you who have affirmed my deepest insights and convictions. It is true that God will turn the world upside down to give his creature-child what she needs and, indeed, there is something awe-inspiring in the way God brought you and me together, so different in background and temperament, and in the way God leads us—brought us together from the ends of the earth.

So now I must begin my story on this lovely day in May, my mother's anniversary. Mother, you too have no need of this book. You read all that is in it and much more besides in the heart of God.

1

YOUR MERCY GREETS ME

I was born into this world with a tortured sensitivity. For long I have puzzled over the causes of my psychological anguish. I think the explanation in great part lies in heredity, possibly aggravated by circumstances. I will try to clarify this.

I must speak of my dear parents. It would be impossible to express how deeply I loved them, with a love which refused to take notice of faults or flaws even though I knew they were there. To me they were 'Mother' and 'Daddy' and those words were weighted with indefinable emotions of trust, love, sureness of keeping. Not until I was an adult could I bear to look on them objectively and estimate them as human persons. This is my story, not theirs, so I will say no more than is relevant.

My mother recognised the tortured side of me but was completely incapable of entering into it, as no doubt she was incapable of understanding it in my father. There was nothing hard about my mother. She was an ocean of tenderness. I am sure she suffered numbly and dumbly before the suffering which was such a mystery to her. I think one of the reasons why she 'hit out' at times was just her own pain at seeing herself helpless to help. As for my dear father, I am sure he did not understand himself and had not come to terms with himself. A man of his generation and class had neither time nor opportunity for being sensitive and still less for the luxury of self-analysis. I am sure he was a painful mystery to himself. To all appearances he was a strong man, very much head of the family. As a child I felt utterly safe when Daddy was around and terrified when he was out of the house. In my early childhood he was the embodiment of safety. The rude awakening did not come until the outbreak of war when I realised that he was, now, powerless to protect us. Yet underneath this exterior was a quivering sensitivity like my own, probably all the more painful in that it was concealed from him and its manifestations must have been inexplicable and humiliating.It is a pain to me now that I did not understand him better. I was the one who could have helped him. As it was, much as I loved him, I had no real intimacy with him.

I, third child of a family of eight, seemed to unite in myself the two sharply differing temperaments of my parents. I suspect that each faced in me the mystery of the other which left each suffering. As I have said, I am sure my mother could not comprehend the manifestations of my father's sensitivity. Not comprehending them she would misinterpret them. On his side my father would shrink from showing her his hidden fears even if he were aware of them. They loved one another deeply, of that I have no doubt, and time was to reveal it unambiguously, but inevitably there were tensions, tensions which reached a climax when I was sixteen. This state of tension aggravated my inborn fears.

Also, my position in the family was unfavourable for an over-sensitive child. Little more than twelve months divided us children from one another. When I came on the scene my mother already had her hands full. I was just twelve months old when James was born. The stage of intense cuddling was over for me then. I suspect that I needed more than my ordinary share and possibly received less than the others. Was it that I seemed reserved and independent? I can remember looking on, not with jealousy—(I cannot remember feeling jealous of any member of my family. I think the deep tenderness which bound me in the flesh to my brothers and sisters ruled out the possibility of jealousy. They were part of me)—but with longing. I longed to be cuddled and hugged. Looking back on my childhood I must single out fear as the preponderating emotion as far as I can recall. My dreams as a child were terrifying. The prevailing one was of hurtling, sliding down a green, slimy, dark abyss. Was this a memory of birth itself? My mother told me that my birth was difficult and that she was ill. I was put aside and, to use her own word, 'neglected', whilst attention was given to her. There is something awe inspiring in recalling the moment of one's birth. Human birth! I wish I could speak adequately of this deep mystery. I can do nothing but recall the unutterable wonder that God too had a

6

human birth: he came into the world as we come into it; he came to drink with us the bitter cup of humanness. He drank it to the dregs and thereby transformed its bitterness. Bitter it is still and yet sweet, for his lips meet ours over the brim.

For me there were bogeys hidden in every dark corner, in everything untested and untried. I would scream and kick with terror when, quite unwittingly, those in charge of me introduced me to some new experience. I was a lively child, bright and gay. Suddenly, inexplicably, in the midst of gaiety, I would dissolve into a flood of tears. Mine were not quiet, unobtrusive ones. On the contrary, they were vociferous and accompanied by fighting, spitting, scratching. Looking back I would say that almost always my tantrums were nothing but fear and wounded sensitivity. Someone unthinkingly trod on my toes; a sense of menace, perhaps due to a passing cloud or a darkening atmosphere, would suddenly descend on me. In my defencelessness I reacted with violent storms.

My father used often to take us out for picnics or drives into the country. Invariably I would post myself at the back window of the car so that I could watch for any lions or tigers that might burst out of the woods and warn Daddy to drive faster. I told no one of these fears, fears which changed their character as the years went by. By the time I was nine years old it was terror of being kidnapped for I had heard talk of kidnappings and murders. I feared bridges and staircases collapsing. Going up in a lift, being on second floors of big stores I clung in terror to my mother's hand. I remember that, even at eleven years of age, venturing on to a pier at the seaside, I disgraced myself, giving way to terror as soon as I saw the sea beneath the slatted boards. I clung, big girl that I was, to my mother, hiding my face in her coat until we reached the end where the band was playing. She sat me in a corner, covering my eyes with a newspaper so that I could not see the water all about us.

There was another side to my character which came more into evidence as I grew older. I 'had character', as they say. I could get my own way and was shrewd enough to act a part for this end. I have just said that I claimed the right to kneel at the back window of the car. This was never disputed. Likewise, I claimed a special place at table. The whole family understood that this was mine and by unspoken agreement it was given to me. I kept it for years. On the mile and a half tram ride which took us daily to the primary school, I claimed the privilege of standing in the conductor's place, up against the radiator, in cold weather. Rarely was this forbidden me by the conductors, who knew us well.

As I grew older I defended myself, hitting back in spite of humiliating outbursts of tears. An instance of this comes to mind. One day in class I was reproved for something and called out in front of the class of boys and girls. I was about six. This bitter humiliation reduced me to a state of impotent rage. I lifted up my frock to hide my face in shame showing all that was underneath. I remember that I was sufficiently mistress of myself to know that all was well beneath; that I had on a very pretty pair of knickers. The teacher gently reproved me but with a touch of hidden laughter in her voice which infuriated me the more. I proceeded to take off my dress and would have done so had she not come to my rescue, gathered me up in her arms with a loving laugh. She often helped me. I think that she more than any other in my early childhood, understood me. She was a personal friend of my mother's. She noticed my fears and would take me into the bogey haunt showing me that it was, in fact, quite empty. Miss Ward, the infants' teacher of whom I have just spoken, who loved us all, told me that I was an ethereal, fairy-like child, and mother has told me that the general feeling was that 'Eve will never rear that child'. My looks belied me. I was highly strung and easily 'run down', needing tonics, ('it is nice to be delicate', I remember sighing when summoned to finish off a bowl of cream), but constitutionally I was hardy. I grew stronger as I grew older and used to wish I could be ill when I saw one of the others having tea in bed with a fire in the bedroom and being called 'poor little lamb' by my mother. Would my time never come? I had to trudge out day after day to school leaving the rest of the tribe snug round the fire with mumps. Mother gave me a chocolate and packed me off. I was not interested in eating. Very soon I was asking to leave the table whilst the others went on enjoying their meal. I was always on the go, lively, restless.

How I loved the countryside! At this stage it was simple delight. It tore my heart as it tears it still to see it spoiled and the lovely meadows, once a sea of grass and flowers, become a building site. Yes, I feel it still and have to argue with myself to get it in perspective. I can bear it in peace only by reflecting that the essence of beauty is eternal and nothing can destroy it. My heart clung with a sort of fanaticism to my simple home and garden. There was a tall hawthorn hedge at the entrance and this enchanted me with its mass of white blossom. Father decided it needed pruning. When I heard he was cutting it down I rushed out and belaboured him with bitter words if not with blows, fuming and weeping. He assured me it would be all the better in a year or two. But a year is eternity to a small child, something defying imagination and without reality. It was the present that mattered, the present with my hawthorn wonder utterly destroyed. Ironically, my father had an equal love for all natural things. He would have been the last to destroy anything. I think he understood my rage; certainly I was not scolded.

As infants, James and I were in the same classroom; in our poor little primary school two classes shared the one room. The infants finished afternoon school earlier than the others and he and I returned home together. It was safe enough. A short walk and we boarded a tram which took us to the terminus at the foot of a steep hill from which branched off the dead-end road at the end of which was our home. From time to time I would find myself without the penny intended for our fare. I was too shy to tell the teacher and preferred to take the risk of stealing a ride. Usually I got away with it. The conductors were kind men, used to us children, and made no fuss. Alas, on one of the penniless rides, an inspector got on and began to ask for tickets. I had none to show. 'Where is your fare?' 'I've left it in my pinafore pocket in the billiard room', I said (the billiard room of the parish club served as the infants' classroom). 'You've got your pinafore on', said James. And so I had, under my coat. The fact was I knew I had lost the penny but did not want to admit that. Secretly I was frightened but put on an air of dignity and in order to indicate to the inspector that I had no more to say, turned my head to the window and began practising my reading, spelling out aloud the advertisements on the placards: B—O—V—R—I—L Bovril. He passed down the line.

Father Christmas visited us every year, of that there was not the

9

slightest doubt. Helena had actually heard the bells of his sleigh! It was only natural that she should be the favoured one. I listened in vain. We had our crib and were told of the Christmas story, but for me it was this kind, mysterious being from another world who made Christmas. It was a wonderful thought. Even at this early age I think I experienced the drabness of life and eagerly welcomed the certainty that this world was not everything; that because there was a Father Christmas and fairies, all sorts of things might happen one day. I began to build my inner world of fairy castles, lovely gardens with magic fruit, flower fairies, elves and secret doors.

If other children told us there was no Santa Claus we knew that he did not visit them because they did not believe. One day, Helena and Mary, rummaging in a cupboard, found some suspicious looking presents which they took to Mother. She assured them that they were intended for the charlady's children, and, in fact, they were. But Helena wept. I think she realised the truth. I do not think I was upset when I knew for the awareness came gradually; besides, I could retire into my own dream world when I wanted to.

I was seven years old when I made my first confession and first communion. They made little or no impression on me. Both parents were faithful catholics. We were taken to mass regularly and taught to say our prayers. Night prayers were part of the family routine. If Daddy was at home he insisted on being called in from the garden. 'Daddy, Daddy, we're going to say our prayers'. He would come in, sit in an armchair, one of us would make a dive for him to 'pray into', one or two would use Mother for the purpose, another Uncle Will. Only one other person was qualified for 'being prayed into' and that was my mother's eldest sister who visited us frequently. In May we had a little altar decorated with spring flowers and we took it in turns to choose a hymn. I can recall no religious impression whatever. Others have told me that God was very real to them in their childhood. I cannot say the same. I knew my catechism and shone at answering all questions on confession, the mass and holy communion, but so far as I know it was not in my heart. Here already is that dryness which has been my lot all my life. What is its meaning? Why is it so? It is too early in my narrative to attempt an answer. Going to bed on the eve of my first communion I felt I should be feeling so different and tried to pray in bed, reciting the hymns we had learned, especially 'Jesus, thou art coming', but alas no feeling came through.

Can a child sin? Until recently I was inclined to answer 'no'. It isn't long since I would say that I found difficulty in taking sin seriously. I meant something like this: We are so blind, so conditioned, our inner drives can be so strong and—most important— God is absent. How then can he be offended when we fail, and still less when a child fails? I myself have known such bitter struggles, have experienced to my depths how weak I am. 'What a God he must be', ran my unexpressed thought, 'to be thus offended. He made us, he knows our nature to the core and what is more, he keeps himself so hidden. How can he expect us to love him and for his sake avoid all evil?' What was I to make of such statements: 'Our sins have crucified our Lord; it was not the soldiers, it was our sins—my sins—that crucified him?' In all honesty I could not say this.

As a little one, preparing for confession, I was conscious of a sort of acting. I had to draw up a list of sins with the number of times. I think I can say with certainty that in my mind I did not in any way relate the items of this list to God, even though I called them sins.

Lately I have come to realise that my notion of sin has been too limited. I thought of sin as a deliberate offence against God, a partial or total rejection of him. Of this I could not consider a child capable and I would even question if anyone is capable of it. Are we big enough? But now I see that it is a mistake to restrict sin to specific and somewhat outstanding acts, as though the rest of our acts (and inactivity is act) when not God-centred are neutral. Rather is sin to be seen as an orientation, a more or less continual series of choices against what one knows in one's deepest heart is right. It is an evasion of life, a refusal to stand in the truth of one's being. This is the offence to God, that his beloved creatures, to whom he longs to give himself, refuse this gift. This gift of his love is enshrined in the acceptance of ourselves and in life as it really is. I hope to show in my story how God in his mercy so arranged my life and enlightened my spirit as to bring home to me the primal obligation to be real, and to see how, in all manner of ways, we human beings shirk this fundamental summons to stand in the truth. 'My life is in my hands';

11

this is true of each of us. I can treasure every drop of my life or I can squander it, letting it drip through my fingers as something of no account.

Distorted images of God imprinted on the mind of a child are hard to eradicate later on. Not only are they imprinted on the mind but embedded in the emotions, in the very flesh, and though the adult mind has purified its ideas, the emotional 'feel' of God secretly tyrannises, if not to affect moral conduct, at least to poison the well-springs of joy. I am making my eighth year a halting-place to look backwards over the road covered, before speaking of Helena and her death in my ninth year. Already, within me, there was an image of myself as ugly and disgusting. I think I was born with this wound; I think it is just part and parcel of extreme sensitivity. Never for a moment did I question my parents' love, it was taken for granted and never reflected on, just like the air I breathed. Whether I was good or bad, I belonged to Mother and Daddy and they wanted me. I think that the sheer secrecy of my inner world, the fears, the nightmares as well as the conscious day-dreaming shut me off from them. Perhaps I instinctively knew that my inner world would never be understood, that if it were revealed I would be condemned. I had no reason for thinking this and I am sure I never consciously thought it, it was but a subconscious knowledge.

'A little closed world of fear and pain'. And no one had the skill in those days to penetrate it. A temperamental, whimsical, difficult but essentially lovable child is what I must have seemed. I had a great capacity for enjoyment but the slightest shadow and my mood changed. I was affected by all sorts of trivial things of daily life. The Monday morning feeling depressed me until the time I entered Carmel: another week beginning, the smell of washing, a hashed-up dinner of cold meat because there was no time to cook, Mother tired; Friday, cleaning day, carpets up, a sense of dreariness and homelessness. On the other hand, I knew quiet ecstasy, sitting in the rich, uncut grass of the lawn beneath an arch of rambler roses, gazing at a shiny birthday card I had received. A tiny child does not reflect back and forth, it takes life as it comes. It seems to me it is precisely this lack of reflection which gives such pathos to a child's suffering.

12

The eldest of the family and 'flower of the flock' she was called, and to me Helena was something of a goddess. I expect I knew that she was Mother's 'dream-child' as she afterwards told me. I knew she was quite special to Mother and this in no way aroused jealousy. Helena was a being apart with whom there could be no rivalry. Tall for her age, with dark brown curly hair and blue eyes, she was a gracious figure, and it is hard for me now to realise that when she died she was only a child of eleven. Instinctively I think of her as a girl of fifteen or sixteen for so she seemed to me at the time. I do not know whether in fact her top lids were straight and therefore veiled her eyes ever so slightly, but that is the impression I have. She was always merry but from time to time, when thoughtful and quiet, her eyes seemed half-veiled, not in a sleepy way but with a sense of mystery. I can see her now when she had become Mother's 'little help', her long slender arms around one of the babies on her knee, her fair brown head and lovely face bent over it. She was my governess, taking me to school and supervising me generally.

In the May of my ninth year, I went into the nursing home for adenoids and tonsils. Secretly I was pleased that it was my turn for getting the fuss. I remember everything very distinctly; the kind Sister, my pretty dressing gown, the theatre, the anaesthetic, and I hurtling through a deep blue starry sky in my pyjamas, with a rushing, roaring sound. My first meal was an embarassment. I knew well that a well-brought-up child like myself should not be fussy over meals but as ill-luck would have it, raspberry sponge was served. I looked at it in dismay and was unable to touch it. Ever since one of our bin-men friends had explained, on being questioned, that the gory mice from traps went to the making of raspberry jam, I could not bear the sight of it. What is more, I noticed something floating in the glass of milk and feared it was a bit of someone's sick. I was ashamed, feeling I was letting the family down, but touch it I could not. There was further embarassment when the surgeon came in to see me and asked me if I liked being in the nursing home. I answered with a decided: 'No, I want to go home'. This was repeated by a lady in the same room to the Sister who was so kind to me. I was upset. In the evening Mother came to see me. I felt she was worried and she spent a lot of time talking to the Sister about Helena who,

13

apparently, was not well. Next day I was due home. I kept my eyes on the drive which I could see through the window, waiting for Daddy to drive up. I felt that I could not wait a moment longer. I was wrapped in a rug and he carried me down and out to the car in his strong arms. Mother was with him and little Brenda. I was conscious of the atmosphere and felt sad. I had wanted to feel very special, to be petted and to have lots of ice cream as Sister had said. Alas, there was no time for me. I was put to bed for a few days. Helena was in the next room. I heard men's voices which I came to realise were the doctors'. And so this day went on. Mother came into me but could not stay and I wept a little. Then the truth became known that Helena was very ill. My good aunts offered to look after us so as to leave Mother free to nurse her. My grandfather and two aunts lived on the same road. We were wonderfully cared for but I was troublesome and always quarrelling with my aunt. One day I ran off, determined to go back to Mother. I was met on the way by Mother's sister who sent me back with a sharp rebuke for being so troublesome when Mother was worried and Aunty was being so good to us. I went back ashamed.

The illness dragged on for six weeks and that seems eternity to a child. We were separated from Mother. We saw her but knew she hadn't time for us. I understood. I remember being allowed to see Helena from time to time. She looked weak and pale and too tired to say more than a few words. Once she told me she had been watching me play on the big rocking horse away on the bit of spare land which we glorified by the name of 'field'. I knew she could be watching me so had played my best, showing-off to my heart's content, leaping into the saddle like a knight, leaping off again.

Grandfather had given us a shilling each. I bought a propelling pencil for my aunty—costing sixpence. The other sixpence I spent on a few narcissi for Helena. I expected to be given a lovely big bunch but alas, such a poor bouquet it looked. Later Mother took me to see Helena. In a weak voice she thanked me for the lovely flowers I had given her. I could not speak for fear the tears I was choking back would overflow. I controlled myself always. I never gave way to storms of tears. I knew Mother was weighed down. I understood.

As the weeks went by, I began to have a strange experience. Walking home from school with a friend on a bright, sunny evening, I would feel that I was lifted out of my surroundings. The familiar road, once so hard, solid, 'there', now seemed alien and remote. This feeling would last for some time. One evening, we saw a crowd and heard a most dreadful sound. Two dogs were fighting to the death. The feeling of 'going away from myself' became intense but I gave no sign of it. It would occur at other times in a less acute form. At this time, Miss Ward would occasionally come with us to tea at Grandfather's. I was always glad to have her. She and Aunty took us for a walk in the country. After a while they encouraged us children to go ahead with one another. Although I did so, realising that they wanted to talk together, I tried to hold back so as to catch what they were saying. I knew they were talking about Helena. I cannot remember all that I heard but I do remember them speaking of my mother's grief and my aunt saying that she had seen my daddy 'crying all day at work'. My heart was constricted. I found myself walking on as in a dream, wondering if anything was real.

We came back, had tea and began to wash the tea things with Miss Ward. By this time, I really felt as if I was leaving myself and could stand it no longer but shrieked: 'Miss Ward, Miss Ward, I'm dying!' Miss Ward turned towards me, eyes, mouth open, took her hands from the sink and held them out to me: 'Darling, you're not'. She clasped me in her arms and kept me imprisoned at her side, walking me up and down the garden. Contact with her body and her warm personality restored me. I think my mother must have been told for from then on I slept at home. Lying in bed one night, before it was dark, it happened again. I tried to endure it, instinctively knowing that Mother would be cross. But I could not and cried out: 'Mother, Mother, I am dying'. Helena's weak voice joined mine from across the passage: 'Mother, Ruth says she is dying'. There was a note of mockery in her voice, or so it seemed to me. My poor mother came running upstairs, kindly brusque and matter-of-fact, told me not to be a silly girl, blessed me with holy water, tucked me up and left me. I am sure it must have been nearly the last straw for my mother's stretched nerves and breaking heart. I cannot explain this experience. I can only suggest that it was the expression of acute loneliness and isolation.

After five or six weeks of pain and semi-starvation, Helena was taken to hospital for an operation. My parents fully expected the Sisters to take her into their nursing home and I know Mother felt it deeply when they pleaded they had no bed. She was convinced that it was because they considered the chances of survival minimal and, in the early years of their establishment, wanted to avoid what might seem a failure on their part. My paternal grandmother had died in their home. Mother dreaded her precious child being swallowed up in the impersonal, institutional atmosphere of a large hospital. Her fears were unfounded. Thanks to the doctors who had followed the course of the illness with the greatest concern and compassion, she was put in a little room, and was happy. Nurses passing by would call in to have a word with her. Mother spent many hours there. The operation was hailed as a marvellous success. But, worn out with the weeks of pain and starvation, the heart failed and she lay dying. 'The hospital is ringing with my praises over that operation', said the catholic surgeon, 'and the child lies dying. That shows who is master of life'.

On the day Helena died I was unwell and Mother kept me away from school. Consequently I picked up snatches of conversation, and gradually the awful truth was penetrating my mind. I heard my aunt say that Uncle Will had been sent for. The afternoon was sultry and breathlessly hot. The sense of oppression bore down on me. Something terrible was happening! At last I heard a car and dashed to the front of the house. It was the parish priest's car. It stopped and Mary and the others got out. Mary was crying. I ran down the pathway, my heart in my mouth, trying to utter: 'How is Helena!'. 'She's dead', replied Mary.

My mother hid her grief and gave herself to us unstintingly, allowing no sense of gloom to pervade the home and in no way restraining the children's good spirits. Only Mary and I were really aware of her loss. Mother explained that we would not have the usual party this year, but we should have one next year, and that was all. I was very conscious of her sorrow. Her eyes would fill with tears whenever Helena's name was mentioned. Rarely did we speak of her and any details I have recounted I learned at the time. I gained hardly any more information for I could not bring myself to question Mother. Trying to comfort her before leaving home for Carmel, I stupidly remarked that time lessens sorrow and that she would get over the separation. 'It is nine years since Helena died and I have not got over that. You can't get over these things', she replied gently without any bitterness.

Helena's death left me scarred. Later someone was to suggest that I had never forgiven God for taking her. Forgiveness implies a sense of personal relationship and, with God, I was conscious of none. He was too much God for that. What is more, I never heard from either of my parents anything to suggest that God had wronged us, not the least complaint or note of rebellion, only words indicating unquestioning acceptance of his will. They turned to him for comfort and it was obvious that they found it. I think my attitude was more like this: 'Nothing is safe any more. Anything terrible can happen, it has happened once and can happen again and there is no one can stop it. God won't stop it.' The menace had taken form and substance and I connected this with God. He had not intervened to save Helena though we had prayed to him. Indeed, it was he who had taken her from us, everyone said so. He was a terrible God. Engraven on my flesh was the feeling of God as the one who deprived, who was jealous of our human loves. Let me love anyone and God was sure to remove my loved one. This wound was only later healed by a friend God gave me, a friend who loved me with a deep love and in whom I have found joy. The trouble was on an emotional level and God came to me on the emotional level through friendship.

17

2
YOUR HAND UPON ME

A new era of my life began at nine years old ending at eighteen with my entrance into Carmel or perhaps a year and a half earlier with my 'conversion'. It was an era of conflict and painful searching. If hitherto I had accepted life, its wounding harshness, unreflectingly, now I began to reflect, to resent, to rebel. My shrinking sensibility sought defences and escapes; my powerful, creative nature to dominate and control the flow of events. A clearly-defined conflict emerges between egotism and love of my family, with the growing victory of the latter. I begin to question the meaning of life and God is put in the dock.

The summer after Helena's death, my vital energies were poured into playing the boy. Long-legged, slim, I was an excellent runner and joined the boys in their games. Our neighbourhood abounded in children and we formed what we called 'our gang'. I had heard Mother speaking with admiration of an Eton crop she had seen. That was enough for me. I demanded one. I tended to identify with Mother. This, I think, was the prime reason for the crop, but there was also the craving to be singular, to take a risk and be outstanding. I soon regretted this hasty decision but was too proud to admit it. I was not indifferent to pretty dresses and wreaths and saw the incongruity of a boy's head sticking out of frills, and still more, crowned in a wreath of marguerites! I played and tumbled with the boys, coming home with bloody chin and forehead for which Mother had no sympathy. I must excel. I expected to be beaten by the boys but resented being beaten by a girl. When I knew I was likely to be outstripped I would not enter the lists. My father pointed this out to me and sheer shame forced me into accepting defeat gracefully.

Even normal, everyday things which others could take in their stride were a burden to me. When my mother told me of menstrua-

19

tion my reaction was one of tearful anger: '*That*, every month! It isn't fair', I cried. Mother reproved me sharply: 'Every woman has it, why should you be different. You have to accept it like everyone else. Our Lady had it'. This latter point was a real comfort to me. Later, in Carmel, I was made to understand that, in fact, she did not. This exemption was implied in the virginal conception. It was a cruel blow. Needless to say, I rejected this false notion as soon as I had investigated sufficiently. I have always found, not merely comfort, but inspiration and ever-growing appreciation of womanhood from the true womanhood of Mary. Mother gave me no understanding of the nature and purpose of menstruation. As fas as I knew it was just an unfair imposition. God did it. He needn't have made us like that. Why did he make things so ugly and difficult? Thus ran my secret thoughts which, with my catholic upbringing, I could not utter. Menstruation was another of my miseries not resolved until I entered Carmel. Mother never allowed us to think that we had reason to feel unwell and I do not think it occurred to me to connect headache, fatigue and general malaise with an oncoming period. But the misery lay in not knowing how to manage during a long day at school, terror lest something should happen in public, games, swimming, the discomfort and chafing. I used to see others seemingly so carefree and wonder how they managed. I was too shy to tell Mother of my difficulties.

When Mary was considered old enough to make the long journey across the city, we were taken away from the primary school and sent to the convent high school, Mary, Betty and I first, Margery, Brenda and Crispin the following term. James had been sent, some years before, to the catholic boys' secondary school. Looking back, I think of the poor little primary school with affection. It was part of the home situation, bound up with the parish and the people I knew. There was a homely, personal tone even though the standard of teaching left much to be desired. Mother had tried to supplement this. She bought us interesting books and we would have reading sessions together of prose and poetry. She would ask us questions and set tests for us. I enjoyed anything in the literary field but when it came to sums, no!

The convent school seemed huge and teeming with girls. At the primary school we had been leading lights, here we were nobodies. Perhaps this was one of the reasons why I was unhappy. I was lost in a crowd. I was shy, felt inadequate, awkward, ugly with a band across my teeth and a plate in my mouth which prevented clear speech. The headmistress, Vim we called her, was a stern disciplinarian. We were terrified of her. To be sent to Vim was about the worst punishment anyone could devise. Later on I was to discover the diamond hidden under this rough exterior, the store of warm, selfless love carefully concealed. Perhaps, even in those early years, I had a glimpse of the true person. My mother thought the world of her and this influenced me.

School and home were two different worlds for me and I had the feeling that school was a threat to home. I am sure the supposed hostility was a product of my own mind. I suspect it lay in the impersonal nature of so large an establishment. Myself, my sisters and my parents were not sufficiently valued. What is more, at school I was not myself. I was too frightened to relax and express myself; too frightened to apply myself to work and it was some years before my abilities began to show. Of course there were happy times and delightful people at school but all my affection and loyalty were centred on my home. As often as not my father would come to take us home. Mother was invariably waiting for us, a cooked tea ready. We would sit down happily, eight children and Mother and Daddy and Uncle Will. Daddy would ask us about the day and we would chatter on. If one of us had been in trouble we carefully avoided reference to it, leaving it to the delinquent to tell Mother herself or, if we felt she had been unjustly treated, one of us would tell her on the quiet. We knew we would get no sympathy whatever if we had been at fault or impertinent in any way.

After tea came homework, all of us sitting round a big table in the drawing room. Mother was sure to look in whilst we were at work. Oh, how dear she was! She was the sunshine of the home and queen of our hearts. Certainly she was queen of mine. We were so proud of her. She was always beautifully dressed with her snow-white hair softly waved. Once I overheard friends remarking: 'She is very nice, but isn't she old?' This hurt me. I had never thought of Mother as old, but of course, comparatively, she was. Helena's illness and death had aged her in appearance but in heart she was one of us. 'Where's Mother?' was everyone's question from Father downwards, if her presence was not immediately evident. I know we all felt the house was empty on the rare ocasions she was not there.

In the spring and summer, on Sundays or holidays, Father would take us to the sea for the day or, more delightfully from my point of view, to the country. Within a few miles of home there was an amazing variety of landscape; moorlands of heather, bilberry and spiked grasses, steep slopes deep in bracken, vividly green valleys with swift running brooks and rivers, woodlands and pasture. Often we would go hiking and Mother would come too, and often we would overreach ourselves. Then we must make for the nearest tavern and ring for Daddy to come and pick us up. They live in my memory, those golden days of beauty and perhaps most of all the heart-breaking sweetness of the bluebell woods.

We were fond of theatricals, although I think it would be more correct to say that I was fond of theatricals and roped in my younger sisters and brother. I wrote the plays, produced them and played a leading part. I would so bully my cast that, one by one, they would leave me in indignant tears saying they 'wouldn't be in it'. There was nothing for it but to go to Mother and ask her to persuade them to come back. This she invariably did but counselling me to be gentle and kind to them. I tried, if only to ensure the success of the play, but I think too I began to learn how to handle people. The play was produced on Christmas night for Mother, Daddy and Uncle Will. James, who whilst we were practising must needs be off playing with his pals, on Christmas night itself, there being no question of other diversions, wanted to take a part, so we would improvise one for him. He would help us too with the lighting effects. Mary rarely acted, as she quickly assumed the role of the grown-up. She would play the piano to accompany the singing. As soon as the play was over Daddy was sure to say:'It was too short, let's have it all over again'.

At twelve years of age a newcomer joined our gang. Two years older than most of us, I found him different from the other boys. What is more, he treated me quite differently. I suddenly realised that I was a girl, a young woman. The desire to excel in games, to beat the boys, died away. Andrew would treat me as if I were made of china, never bowling me out, helping me off a wall, always making me precede him through a gate. We were in love. This was no child-affection; it was passion. There was deep, intuitive recognition of the other, not the slightest doubt of our immense importance to one another. I had a respect for myself that was altogether new, knowing myself loved in this way. The world was transfigured. Andy was my world. I felt that I could not live without him. He was in my thoughts night and day. Years later, mother's sister recalled an afternoon I had spent with her and all my conversation had been of the wonders of Andy. When he was absent I lived for the moment of his coming and would stand on the bank where I could see the trams coming into terminus, watching for his wiry figure to leap off the tram with a twist all his own, and run up the hill.

The gang accepted this love-match quite simply, except that they were annoyed when our games went awry because of his partiality for me. But nearly always we were on the same side and this was taken for granted. Unashamedly we would walk along, our arms around each other's neck, our playmates quite content for us to be a little way ahead or behind. Sometimes, tired with our play, we would throw ourselves on the grass to rest and he would lay his head on my chest or I would lay mine on his. I loved to feel his hard, boyish body, so different in feel from a girl's. Once or twice we exchanged shy kisses. I never remember wanting to go off in secret to show or give more of our bodies to one another. There seemed no need to do so. Our love was certain, free, full of mutual respect. I instinctively felt Andy's integrity. I knew I could trust him. He was pure. I never saw or felt anything but what was beautiful. The grown-ups smiled at us but I knew I had to keep Andrew away from my father who became increasingly intolerant of boys coming to the home. This innocent love affair died a natural death through separation. It is still an embarassment to me that something which affected me totally was so short-lived. Just before I entered Carmel I met him again with his fiancée. I felt not the slightest jealousy or desire but looked on him with great appreciation for the fine man he had become.

My love for Andy was unashamed. The whole world could know of it. I find it interesting and significant that my love for a young priest serving in the parish, a love which persisted from about the age of thirteen to sixteen, must be hidden at all costs. Not only must it be hidden, I felt guilty and was ashamed of it. Why? There were no reveries of intimacy which, understandably, could have aroused guilt feelings. It was the love itself which shamed me. Is it that such a love as this—a crush, an infatuation—is felt to be unworthy, not fully human? It is beneath human dignity to be infatuated by another human being, expecting nothing in return. It is an ineffectual passion leading nowhere. I think my pride urged me to conceal this involvement though, needless to say, it was impossible to conceal it fully. It is true enough, no doubt, that crushes are normal in adolescence, a preparation for true love later on; all the same, they are not fully human and must be worked through. True human love contains two elements: a giving, a self-surrender to the beloved, but also a completion in the beloved.

I hope I have written enough to give a picture of the general background against which I was developing. By every standard it was a good, happy home presided over by devoted parents. There was a shadow, imperceptible at first and making no great impression on the conscious mind whatever its effect on the subconscious. I do not want to say much, only enough to give a true picture of my environment. We knew our parents quarrelled and at the time would feel gripped with terror and something like horror. But the storm would pass and the sense of warmth and security return. Yet why were there times when I would lie awake waiting for Daddy's car lights to streak across the ceiling before I could go to sleep? A haunting fear that one day he might not come back? And the same dread when, occasionally, Mother would announce that she was going out. I am sure she merely went to let off steam to her sister but I used to live in fear lest she might not come back. Yet in spite of all this, by far the overall impression was that of security in our parents and I never doubted that they loved one another. It was only later on that this shadow became a veritable nightmare, as I must tell.

As I grew into adolescence the difficulties of my temperament increased and I became a burden to myself and a trouble in the home. A very slight affront, a sharp word, an impatient gesture from my parents would throw me, without warning, into a black mood. Often I would fly into a violent rage and attack with my fists. I could never hurt. No matter how great my rage, my hand fell limp. The rage would be followed by days of sulking. Utterly miserable myself, I tended to make others miserable too. I would stay outside the family circle, morose and sullen. I longed to join in again but was too proud to yield. Sometimes I would refuse to go with the family on their Sunday outings, all the time hating myself because I saw how eagerly and tenderly Mother and Daddy prepared it for us. I hated myself and the more I hated myself the more sullen and depressed I became. I was extremely unhappy and I did not know what was the matter. The world seemed utterly black.

At times I wanted to die; I used to think out how I could run away. However, love of the family always restrained me. I could never have hurt Mother and Daddy to that extent. My father was one of the principal causes of my moods. I think it was because I felt he did not sufficiently recognise my value but looked down on me as he would on a child. And yet I loved him. Even at the time I was behaving so badly I loved him and felt hateful for being so horrid to him. I found it impossible to come back to him as I did to Mother. If I was at odds with her I nearly always ran back when I had taken but a few steps from the house on my way to school, to kiss her goodbye. I remembered the occasions when I had gone off in high dudgeon without being reconciled with Mother. I lived in anguish for the rest of the day fearing Mother might die while I was away and I would not be able to tell her I was sorry and show her that I loved her. I think I was about fifteen when it came home to me how selfish I was; how I was upsetting the family and grieving my mother. I made up my mind to try to hide my feelings or at least, not let everyone else suffer from them. Then began the struggle which has gone on to this day. There were many, many lapses for my moods were tyrannical.

When I question myself as to the basic cause of this depression, sadness and bitter frustration, it is not easy to point to one particular thing. I have said sufficient of my earliest years to show that to a great extent it was inherent in my make-up. Intermingled with this was, I think, a religious problem, as I will tell, but I would suspect that underlying the grief was the ugly self-image. The slightest affront or criticism brought me face to face with it. I hated myself, rejected myself and shut out love. And the more I shut out love, the more I saw myself being bad, the more frustrated and hateful I seemed.

Many, many years later, I witnessed an incident which demonstrated how I might have been helped in this extremely difficult dilemma. My brother brought his little family to the parlour. Without warning, the eldest went to the back of the room and hid her face in the cushion. Some little remark had wounded her. I knew just what she felt like and the sheer knowledge that already she had gone so far as to disgrace herself before Aunty made the situation all the more hopeless. My brother, with tremendous understanding, went over to her quietly, gathered her up in his arms and cuddled her. Her face was flaming with shame and he buried it in his breast. After a little while he brought her over to us, remarking on her lovely plaits. Apparently she was very conscious of her straight hair. She thought it ugly. I was deeply moved by James' understanding and perfect handling of the child. As for the child, I identified with her completely. Alas, no one in my really loving home grasped the inner loneliness of the difficult child that was me. I think if Mother or Father had come over to me and put their arms round me I would have burst into helpless tears that would have been my healing. I was not scolded. I was just left to get over it. The family circle was always wide open and at the first sign I was welcomed, but I had to make the first move and it was this which was so appallingly hard. This trouble is with me still. I still have to resist the feeling of panic which arises when I am in any way criticised or found to be at fault.

I was growing plump and bursting my dresses. Mother did not find it easy to keep up with our quick growth for the school uniform was expensive. One day at assembly I found myself without kneeling-room, and self-conscious as I was, knelt down anyway just to be inconspicuous. We had our backs to Vim on the rostrum. Her voice called out: 'Who is that great fat lump?' I had a sickening feeling that I was. 'Turn round, let me see who you are'.

When I was in fifth form, to add to my general sense of misery, my eyesight became defective and I had to wear glasses. I thought I was plain enough without having a pair of tortoise-shell spectacles stuck on my nose. Many a time I wept in secret over them.

It might appear that I had devout ideas and feelings. This is not so. I was conscious of a sense of hypocrisy when I wrote religious poems, realising that the Sisters at school and others would be impressed and think me rather special. This fact gave me some pleasure but essentially it embarassed me. Certainly I did not write to impress. I was beginning to feel that there was nothing worth writing about except God and yet there was not the slightest feeling of him. I began to look for words about him in all sorts of books. I rummaged on the religious shelves of the public library, peeping with a creepy fear into non-catholic books but refraining from reading them as this was forbidden. I found something of Fr Faber's but cannot remember what it was.

Between the ages of thirteen and fourteen, I began to wonder about God. Did he really exist? Did I not believe just because I had been brought up to believe as I had believed in Father Christmas? When, later on, we read more freely in history, and when I began to realise that seemingly the majority of people, clever people, did not believe in him, the doubt gained in impetus. Added to this was a growing sense of the meaninglessness of life. Hitherto I had taken things for granted. Home was solid, a sheer *must be* that even the ominous warnings I had received failed to shake, but now I realised with piercing grief that it was not so. One day Mother and Daddy would die. One day, not very far away, I must leave home. I would go to Oxford, teach, marry, and then...? Then death. The thought of death as the end of all things became very real to me. I could tell no one of my unhappiness.

From fourth form onwards my immediate ambition was to win a state scholarship which would take me to Oxford. This ambition had nothing to do with an academic career but with the romantic desire for 'the city of dreaming spires'. I wanted to escape from the industrial cities to what was almost another world of ancient colleges, cathedrals and 'silver streaming Thames'. I kept my secret to myself, for at this time there was little to indicate that I had the ability. I was quite sure I had. I never doubted but that, if I worked reasonably hard, I would win the scholarship. In some ways I was extremely self-confident and probably over-assessed my capabilities.

27

Beyond this romantic dream lay a much deeper one, the longing to marry. No, it could not be anyone of my own station, no one I could see around me, but someone quite special. It is hard for me to recapture what I had in mind, what my idea of marriage was. It was love. I wanted to be utterly loved by someone, loved uniquely. Children were not essential. It was the companionship, the love which was my longing. At the back of my mind was the uncomfortable awareness that there was another state of life, that of the consecrated virgin. I turned away from this and supported myself with the reading from Proverbs of the valiant woman, which I found as the lesson of the mass for a woman saint not a virgin. Part of my desire to go to Oxford was the hope of meeting someone who would fall in love with me and want to marry me.

At fifteen I was conscious of myself as growing up. Many, many times I had looked into the mirror, now this way, now that, trying to see if there was anything about me that could be called beautiful but it seemed quite certain there was not. At fifteen I was not so sure. Sometimes when I caught myself in a certain light it was a delicate, rather lovely face that looked back at me. I was delighted. But take a step back into another light and I was little better than a turnip— broad-faced, stodgy, strained. I consoled myself with the thought that perhaps others saw the first image, and it would seem that, at home at any rate, this was so. My relatives and my former playmates made me feel that I was attractive. I was clever. I grasped that it was precisely the image of the pure, fresh young girl growing into womanhood which appealed and I took care to preserve it. 'Standing with reluctant feet/Where the brook and river meet'. O yes, I was clever enough to see this. I avoided the least sophistication and seemingly was indifferent to dress. Simplicity was my keyword. I chose my first long dress. It was white organdie with a little crimson trimming! Yes, I was rather satisfied with myself that Christmas as I gazed into the mirror in the soft glow of candlelight.

The war was drawing to a close and my father and mother decided to send us to boarding school. My father foresaw that he would be obliged to go abroad in two or three years' time, in which case the younger children would have to board. My parents considered that separation from home coinciding with settling in a foreign country would be too much for them emotionally and therefore the separation should come now whilst Mary and I were still at school with them. Furthermore, in the previous year, Vim had resigned her post as headmistress of the day school, finding so big an institution beyond her strength, and was now in charge of a small boarding school of a few years' standing, about thirty miles from the city. So greatly did my parents esteem this nun that they wanted us still to be under her guidance and were far from satisfied with the state of the day-school since her departure.

I was upset by my parents' plans although I could understand their motives and that, at bottom, they were seeking only what was best for us. I hated the idea of boarding school and I let off my repressed resentments on the school. I was bitterly homesick. Hitherto I had been able to escape from the tyranny of the school. It was left behind each evening and we entered the loved world of home. Now there was no escape. It was school all the time. I hated it, hated being part of an institution, resented the loss of independence and the complete control of the school authority.

Our parents came to see us every Sunday afternoon but Mary and I took it in turns to go home each Friday evening to be with Mother. The tensions between my parents were heightening. We children had been their bond of union and common devotion. Now we were gone. Mother was lonely, for the house had suddenly become a desert. Father gave his time and energy to his big project and understandably she felt neglected. I was deeply affected by this conflict. My sympathies were with my mother. I could read every line of her dear face and knew how hurt, humiliated and lonely she felt. I was desperate to be with her and yet my presence could have been small comfort seeing how distraught I was. But I loved my father and was torn with pity for him even though he angered me. It was obvious he was unhappy and was just throwing himself into activity to escape from himself. I am sure that a good adviser could easily have put things right between them, helping each to understand the other, for I had proof over and over again how deeply they cared for one another. It was precisely because they cared that they hurt one another and suffered so much. Alas, in those days they would never have dreamed of seeking professional help.

The coming of spring brought an easier aspect to life at school. I had always longed to live in the country and here I was doing so. The lovely old manor house, which formed the nucleus of our school building, lay in a valley. A swiftly flowing river, coursing over a rocky bed, sang day and night below our windows and small mountains rose beyond. All around was fertile pasture land, marked off with green hedges. It was a sheep-rearing district and the slopes of the hills and dales were dotted with sheep. Daffodils grew in wild profusion to be followed later by bluebells. We spent lovely hours in the valley or among the hills by the clear mountain streams. I had made friends with a girl of my own age, Sylvia, and she was able to share my emotional response to nature.

3

YOU ARE MINE

Often I have complained in my heart that God seemed absent from my life. It seemed to me that I had to live life all alone, eating it in its raw bitterness. He was not there to give me understanding and comfort. Even now I can sympathise with myself over this. A hidden God he has been to me, but God indeed.

Faith tells me he is in every event. At every moment of existence, 'from my mother's womb you are my God'. But it is possible to detect more clearly defined indications of his presence and activity; and there are moments fraught with deeper consequences. I was left, it seems, struggling with the misery of my temperament and yet, thanks in great part to a loving home, gradually choosing to do right. Inevitably I would seek to escape from the drab misery of life as I experienced it by living in a world of fantasy, and yet I was made to realise the falsity of this activity and to renounce it. No one instructed me in this. No one understood me enough to counsel me. The light came from within my own heart. Again I was given light to see my selfishness in inflicting my moods on my family and again I chose right.

I have spoken of the strong romantic elements in my nature. It is true that this can lead to unreality but it can likewise point to truth. In my case it was a profound dissatisfaction with life. I was looking beyond and above, waiting for the secret door to open, waiting for the beloved to appear and transform my life. I tended to approach life with intense expectancy, wanting to extract from it the last ounce of sweetness, only to be bitterly disappointed, finding it insipid if not downright sour.

This is a common experience, and no doubt some would consider it pathological. Everything depends on how the inmost heart reacts. One can 'opt out' and choose to live divorced from reality, refusing

31

to play any constructive part in the community, or one can accept this dissatisfaction as a goad urging one to seek the truth, to seek the ultimate, the true meaning of life. I could say that, almost unconsciously, I was being led to choose the latter course. The age of thirteen to sixteen represents, I think, a very truthful era of my life. I was struggling, unhappy, lonely; life was grim, and yet I had deliberately refused to escape from it. It is true that there was a measure of playacting at school but this was superficial. It was my home-self which I acknowledged as my truth. It was at home that I showed myself in my true colours with my dreadful moods and outbursts. And it was at home that my chief battles were fought. Here I made efforts to be unselfish, to be thoughtful and helpful towards my parents. Here I learnt to be sensitive and kind to others. Sensitive myself, I came to be most sensitive towards others, avoiding anything that I knew would wound. There were continual failures, but the struggle was on, and this was, so to speak, 'without God'. I mean I was not consciously trying to please God. I was following an inner light without reference to whence the light came.

I earlier raised the question of why no religious impression got through to me. Why I was so empty and dry at my first communion. Clearly it was not the dryness of sheer indifference, else why was I aware of it, aware that it was incongruous? Why did I set myself to pray, to think about our Lord coming to me? An explanation possibly lies in the self-rejection; in the image I had of myself. Unconsciously I was saying: 'God can't love me. I am not a bit good'. But perhaps too, it lay in capacity. Were not the images of our Lord wholly insipid to me? I think it is true to say that my religious aspirations found outlet in my fairy-tale heroes and, later, in my imaginery but never defined lover-to-be. It seems to me that I was really searching for a person. If my religious teachers had known how to exploit this inner world of mine, it may well be that my heart would have been won consciously for our Lord. As it was, the world of religion was as drab as the real world.

At fifteen years of age I was becoming aware of my gifts and with this awareness came danger, the danger of attempting to deny, live apart from, the shadow side. I was trying—unsuccessfully—to change my self-image. But the odds were against this—happily—

and my temperament too tyrannical. By a strange paradox it was what one would call my religious conversion that became the greatest temptation to unreality, to escape from the truth of my own being. Again, God in his mercy used all my twisted motives and aspirations, drawing me to where there would be no escape, where I would learn in the bitterest suffering and humiliation what I truly am and eventually find peace and joy in that knowledge. And now I must tell of the spiritual awakening. How complex it was. I hope I shall express it truthfully.

Like every catholic girl of my generation, educated at a convent school, I was aware that there was such a thing as 'religious vocation' and that this was, in theory at any rate, highly esteemed. This aspect was the only one that caused the slightest flutter of my heart but it was certainly not appealing enough to turn my thoughts in the direction of a convent. Resolutely I looked towards marriage.

It was a custom in the school for the girls to make a few days retreat annually. It was to take place in the half-term holiday of Whitsun. I was furious, partly because it was taking a slice out of our coveted holiday at home but chiefly because I felt it as an imposition. The nuns had no right to force their piety on us. I resented what seemed to me an invasion of my personal privacy. They had the right to teach us in all manner of ways, but our spiritual life was no affair of theirs, I argued. However, I was too concerned for my good standing in the school and in the opinion of the nuns to stay away. Inwardly smouldering I went. Deliberately I set myself to be a nuisance. I refused to keep silent and chattered to anyone who was willing to chatter. Some of the girls were taking the retreat seriously and our chatter harassed them. I heard not a word of what the preacher said. To this day I cannot remember a single word. Quite suddenly, in the middle of the second day, I was seized with a sense of fear such as I had never known before. It was related directly to God and to him alone. 'What did he think? What was I doing? Wasn't this "resisting grace", and how serious that was.' I went home in the evening still in the grip of this profound emotion, gulped down my tea (there was rhubarb pie and custard which I loved), remarked casually to Mother that I was going off to confession and off I went.

Hitherto I had avoided going to the Canon for confession. He annoyed me with his fussy piety, but now I deliberately went to him. What instinct lay behind this? Was it that, for once, my confession was to be in deadly earnest and that I laid aside all merely personal whims and went to the most experienced priest of the three serving the parish? Something like that, I think. I told him in a very straightforward way what I had done. He asked me why I had behaved so and I replied that I was mad with the nuns. I felt they had no right to be making us pious. He asked was I sure that was the only reason; was I perhaps afraid that God was asking something of me and I didn't want to listen. I assured him quite definitely that it was simply because I was mad with the nuns. I knew what the Canon was hinting at.

I came out of the confessional with a sense of relief and peace. The priest had urged me to spend the next few days well and I was determined to do so. I thought over what he had said. Yes, I knew quite well what he was getting at, hinting that perhaps I had a vocation. I realised that, in fact, I was afraid of being 'good'. That is, if once I decided to be 'good' anything might happen, there would be no knowing where it would end. This was the moment for the grace which changed my life. At the deepest level of my self I *saw* that God existed. He filled life. He offered intimacy to man. It was possible for us to be intimate with God! Bewildering realisation. That being so life could have no other meaning. I must give myself up to seeking this intimacy with God. The self-evident way was to be a nun, a nun in the most absolute way possible, an enclosed, contemplative nun. These successive thoughts were almost instantaneous. All happened in a moment but my mind was made up in the sort of way that it would have been impossible to unmake. My world was completely changed.

So powerful was this grace—it was not experienced in an overwhelming way, rather it was veiled in obscurity and also by a web of natural movements—that it changed me in an instant and radically. It was a real 'conversion'. I was turned right round. I use the passive tense deliberately. It was not I who turned. God turned me. My orientation was henceforth different, it was to him, and so fundamental, radical was this orientation that I think it would have been impossible for me to reverse it or withdraw from the powerful current which now had me in its grip. What others have to come to through steady application and labour, had been done for me in a moment. A work of detachment had been wrought for me. This was a 'short-cut' such as St Teresa speaks of; a mystical grace which of its very nature is efficacious. There has been no other such in my life. From then on I had to submit to the toilsome, slow climb of the ordinary way. This grace was but a beginning. It set me on the mountain, at its base, but so firmly, so surely that it has been, as I say, impossible to withdraw. It would have been necessary to unmake my fabric, so to speak, for that to happen.

But from then on and apart from that, my path lay in darkness, deep darkness; and I had to struggle bitterly for the practice of virtue. Nothing of that was made easy. Yet I think I can say truly that, thanks to this initial grace, not for one hour have I given up the climb. I have known utter dejection and near-despair. I have known intolerable bitterness and yet never have I ceased to turn within to him who, so obscurely, so hiddenly, drew me to himself. Without this special grace I could not have gone to him. Without it I would never have entered Carmel. And what would have become of me? Possibly for some years I would have followed a path of success. Possibly married. But sooner or later the conflict between the two sides of my nature would reach a crisis. Would I have resolved it successfully? It is hard to think so. If I had married, could I, given my afflicted, wounded nature. my supersensitivity, have made a success of it? Again it is hard to think so. It seems to me that my way to God and thus to personal fulfilment in God could only be in Carmel. Only here could I be freed to give myself to God. Here I was subject to a stern discipline which, though it seemed like a cruel straitjacket, strengthened my will, giving it mastery over my emotional instability. Here I faced myself nakedly. Here there were no escapes. Here I learned to accept myself and to trust in God and so find wholeness.

My habit of self-watching and analysis detected simultaneously with this supernatural insight—indeed it was in danger of not giving the latter due importance—the tangle of self-centred strands weaving around the precious core. Here was a way of escaping from the rut. Here a way of being quite special, the centre of attention. Here was the highest, the most refined ambition. How do justice in words to this jumble of contrary movements? First the pure heart of the matter such as I have described, then the feeling 'special' and delighting in this, shame at feeling so, self-despising for the superficial little show-off that I was. Could God really be in this? Had I not 'made it up'? Were it not for the profound effects I would have doubted the reality of the grace itself.

At the time it occurred I was still plagued by religious doubts. For a week or two under the influence of this grace they disappeared completely in the glorious realisation of God's existence. He was totally remote from me. There was no relation between us as yet, but there could be. That was my ambition. Yes, I was going to have those wonderful experiences and feelings which the saints had instances of and which I saw depicted in pictures hanging in the school. Suddenly I was free from the bonds which tied me to my family. I think it would have been quite impossible for me to break them but now they had melted without effort on my part. Every love died in my heart. I wanted no one. I wanted to be alone. I no longer wanted my hitherto inseparable companion, Sylvia. And yet I carefully refrained from giving any sign of this detachment. Deliberately I took the greatest care to show my mother and father all love. After a little while, loving feelings returned, but not in the same way. I was free. This detachment was wrought in an instant without pain. After a short time, too, the feeling that God did not exist returned.

I went back to school to finish the last lap of the summer term with a faint aura round my head. I was no longer subject to moodiness and fits of depression. It was easy to be kind and thoughtful. I was 'special'. I wanted to be alone and spent most of my free time before the blessed sacrament. I was both pleased and embarassed when others came along and saw me there. My prayer as always was utterly blank. If I was tempted to feel I was approaching holiness, the awareness of my conceitedness, my love of attention, playacting and insincerity made me despise myself. I was aware of all sorts of ugly things in me, the desire to be *the* one, to be jealous of others, the tendency to win esteem at all cost. Were not such things incompatible with a vocation? I did not want to claim to be such a creature as that. Was I not the girl with a vocation? Given the basic split in my character, as I hope I have shown earlier, the wounded, sensitive side and the rich, powerful one, a dangerous situation was brewing.

I no longer wanted to go to Oxford and lost interest in my studies. It was hard to apply my mind to anything. When at home for holidays I struggled to hold on to the realism of the supernatural which was in such danger of being submerged in ordinary life. I resisted the appeal of the films which left me with a sense of 'Am I not a fool? This world is so real. Isn't what you are doing quite fantastic?' I was very much alone, but I would keep on turning to God. I was bewildered by the darkness and doubt. Why did I feel like that? Why did nothing happen when I prayed? Of course it was because I was just beginning. What else could I expect? When I had entered, been taught, and done all I should, then it would be different. One day it occurred to me forcefully that it would not be different. It would always be like that. I can remember this moment vividly, the exact spot where I was at the time, so I think I am justified in attaching significance to it. Gradually I began to feel in a realistic way what convent life might be like in practice; the daily, dreary round without romance for which I so longed.

The Lord purified this element even before I entered. Although pathetically maintaining an air of enthusiasm for the life I had chosen to embrace, the inner feeling belied it. If there is a God, I thought, then what I am doing is the best thing I can do. Yes, it will be terribly hard but I shall never turn back. No one can make me fail. I shall go on whatever happens and even the longest life comes to an end and when the end comes how happy I shall be to have lived so. And if there is no God, well, life is worth nothing anyway. There is more sense in assuming that there is and living for him. Strange sentiments for a girl of seventeen, a girl greatly admired and loved, clever, gifted, in the eyes of her entourage 'brilliant' as was said. Few knew of the deep flaws in my nature. And lest I should be under any illusion that the flaws had been healed, an uncontrollable attack of moodiness made me keenly aware of their presence.

I was chosen to be head girl. I had the confidence of the sisters and lay staff as well as of the girls. Vim was to bear witness later to the influence I had exercised in the school. It was at this time I became aware of my power over others. I did not seek power or love in a direct way. I was far too subtle for that. Very independent myself, and hating to be ordered about or treated in an authoritative way, I too refrained from authoritarian or haughty ways. It was known that I fostered no crush, never paid special attention to any one junior but cared for them all. Three younger sisters in the school, equally popular and at the same time devoted to me, added to my prestige and influence. Vim said she had never known a school year like this one. She gave me complete trust, taking me into her confidence over difficult girls, asking me to sit with them at table and help them in any way I could. A troublesome child she would put in my dormitory and invariably I won her. She put me in charge of a dormitory composed of the most difficult girls in the school who, to begin with, had an antagonism for me. I quailed but made up my mind to win them by gentleness and understanding. Within a few weeks they were loving friends. It was a great help to have such a friend as Sylvia. She and I could support one another and thus escape being involved with girls younger than ourselves. But I never held aloof from my sisters. Sylvia more than once remarked that, though we Burrows had lots of friends, we did not really need them; we were sufficient for ourselves. I think this was a true judgement.

I sat for the Oxford entrance examination. I myself, as well as the mistress who tutored me, felt I had done badly. I did not mind. Having no intention of going to Oxford, failing to get the entrance would simplify the issue. I had given up any idea of having passed when, one morning, I received an envelope, opened it at breakfast and could hardly believe my eyes on reading that I had been accepted for Oxford. I burst into tears; I hardly know why.

All told, I have some very happy memories of that last year at school; of beautiful human fellowship, union of heart and mind, real love and a flowering of virtues such as truth, honour, kindness, respect for one another, appreciation and gratitude. I saw characters expand. In all truth I have to say that I was aware of the role I had played in this. All the same, this enormous prestige only deepened the awareness of the miserable creature I really was.

When I told my parents of my wish to be a nun they reacted in the same way as they did over Helena's death. I overheard my mother saying to James: 'If God wants her she must go and that's that.'

Father's reactions were similar but, as always, he looked to Mother in such matters. Her only care was that I should have good direction and go to a convent where I would be well cared for. She was quite appalled when I made it clear that I intended entering an enclosed convent. I tentatively mentioned the Trappistines and at this she wept: 'No, no, you are not cut out for a life like that'. I kept silent from then until I was more sure what I would do.

So I waited for the close of the school year. I received a letter welcoming me to Oxford and enclosing the prospectus. I was not wholly indifferent. It was painful for me to sit down and write to the authorities declining the place. Again, when I heard my school companions and others discussing their plans for the future, I would feel a pang, but all this was superficial and the thought was predominant that I had been given something infinitely better. My companions could never understand. Who could understand except one who has been touched in the same way?

I was still undecided which order I should join. I leaned towards the Cistercians. On the one hand the strong community spirit which, I learned, was a major feature of their way of life, implied a humanness which appealed to me, on the other, fearing the tendency to have a 'crush' and realising that a novice mistress would be a likely victim, the Cistercian's rigid silence seemed a safeguard. But Carmel was beginning to exercise an appeal. Thérèse herself moved me. Here was one, a girl like myself, who had become the intimate friend of God. Somewhere in the appendix of the volume of her autobiography, I came across a reference to the eremitical spirit of Carmel and its demands. This frightened me, I surmised something of the 'desert' involved in such a concept, and yet at the same time it drew me.

My mother asked me to consult a well-known experienced priest. So I laid the case before him telling him I simply did not know which of the two orders I should join. He decided on Carmel. I think the influencing factor was that I told him of Mother's distress at the thought of the Trappistines. Carmel did not seem to frighten her in the same way. The priest arranged to write to the prioress of a newly-founded Carmel of which he had some knowledge. This he did and I was accepted.

Youth is callous. It never occurred to me that I should delay my entrance and stay with my parents for another year or two. I was like a fish out of water and they knew it, and made not the slightest effort to keep me back. Mother hid her grief to such an extent that I began to think she hardly cared. But once or twice, she burst into bitter weeping. I thought my heart would break. Daddy would look at me with his sad, brown eyes: 'So you are going to leave us, Ruthy?' More than once I would wake to find him standing by my bed looking down at me. There was something dumb and helpless about his attitude. Once he followed me into the bedroom and asked if he could see me in the black dress Mother had made for me. Parents make a far greater sacrifice than the prospective postulant. She is going to a new life, the life she has chosen, and for that reason some of the edge is taken off the knife of separation. Not so for the parents. Life for them goes on as usual but with a gaping void.

When the time came for my departure I seemed to be under an anaesthetic. I was numb and unfeeling. After lunch Mother said gently: 'I should get off now dear, there is no point in hanging about'. I knew the heroism behind this sentence. She was trying to save me pain. ('I don't want to make it harder for you', she had sobbed on the occasion of her breakdown). She kissed me in a matter-of-fact way as if I were going to school. I looked around for Daddy but he was not there. Thinking he would be tinkering with the car, I went down the little path. I heard a broken cry and turning round saw him in the doorway with his arms wide open the tears streaming down his cheeks. I ran back and flung myself into his arms. He clutched me to himself in a wild, passionate hug, kissing me over and over again. Mother intervened in her gentle way and released me from his grip. And so I left home in a sort of trance.

4

YOUR FACE I SEEK

I travelled by bus to the Carmel chosen for me by the priest whose advice I asked. I sat alone, I could not speak. If I allowed my thoughts to dwell for a moment on the family the tears would spring to my eyes. I realised that I must keep them out of mind. I had visited the Carmel twice before. My parents had taken me to meet the prioress. It was a strange experience sitting before the grille seeing the tiny, hooded figure on the other side, who eventually raised her veil to show a pleasant, fresh-complexioned face. She spoke gently and reassuringly to my parents and invited questions from me. I was unable to ask any. It seemed to me quite irrelevant what happened or did not happen behind that grille. I had made up my mind to accept all; details were of no consequence. At this visit too I met the tall stately novice mistress and a postulant. The latter fascinated me. I immediately concluded she must be a wonderful person, the 'real thing', conscious all the time that I was not the real thing. Later, Mother, Mary and I attended the clothing of this postulant. The ceremony upset Mother because she thought the postulant looked strained and unhappy.

Well, here I was on September 1st, 1947, sitting on a little stool at the enclosure door waiting for it to be opened. I had received my instructions from the outsister: 'When the door opens you go in, kneel down and kiss the feet of the crucifix and then the hand of our Mother Prioress.' Uncle Will, the last hold on the world that had been mine, stood by. The door ground open, I moved forward into darkness; a few veiled figures stirred in the darkness, I knelt, kissed our Lord's feet and a hand held out to me flicked a piece of cloth before my face, the scapular, no doubt. My eyes grew accustomed to the dimness, veils were thrown back and I was embraced. The novice mistress led me away to my cell where I exchanged my green dress

41

and coat for the black dress Mother had made for me with such care, spending on it more coupons than could be spared and procuring the best woollen material on the market. I was secretly proud of it. She provided me with a handsome silk underskirt as well as a plain sateen one. Alas, the former made such an important swishing sound as I walked that it had to be abandoned.

Looking back now it seems to me an almost incomprehensible thing that I should have done what I did. Here was I resolutely determined never to leave this house I was now entering. House? It was an unknown world of which no one outside could have any real idea. Had I been borne on the wings of a sensible love of God, of enthusiasm or romance, it would have been understandable.

My Carmel was founded a few years before the war. All the nuns, except three who had been received as postulants, and the novice mistress from another community, were from the founding house. With the prospect of making a foundation, subjects had been received indiscriminately, as events proved. The person originally destined to make the foundation, and be its first prioress, died quite suddenly. This upset plans somewhat and, in her stead, M. Teresa was given the task. She was a woman of about sixty years of age, of tremendous nervous energy, with a giant capacity for work, kind but lacking in sensitivity, with little understanding of the highly-strung, nervous character. How often we heard her point out that though she had a store of nervous energy, that was not the same thing as being nervous—a condition she obviously despised. Her idea of the ideal novice or good nun was one who ate heartily, slept well, put on weight, had no conflicts and could work hard. She made efforts to understand those who did not meet these requirements but was often woefully rough and hurtful. Though she came from a well-to-do army family she had received no proper schooling and this was manifest in all sorts of ways, especially in that which mattered most, her grasp of theology and the principles underlying the religious life. There must have been a deep-down awareness of this lack, since she compensated for it by being an authority on everything.

It was only a matter of weeks before I found myself bewildered if not scandalised by her behaviour. Used as I was to the correct and mortified behaviour of the Sisters who had educated me, I found it difficult to think of her as a true nun. I voiced my opinion to the novice mistress, who kindly explained that M. Teresa had not been prepared for the task now thrust upon her, that she was in a most difficult position, but had given herself completely to it and that the community owed her a lot.

The superiors of the founding house, realising that M. Teresa was not fitted for the training of novices and, in any case, would not have the time, had requested a nun suitable for the office from another house. It was quite clear to me that Sr Agnes was of a different breed, conforming to my idea of what a nun should be. She was an intellectual woman with an exceptional education for her generation. On the other hand, she treated her novices rather as school girls—she was not alone in this, it was the accepted attitude—and her instructions were not above fourth or fifth form level of an English school. However, I respected her, for she was a truly faithful nun who practised what she preached. M. Teresa's government must have been a sore trial to her as the two were extremely diverse in background, temperament and outlook, but her obedience was perfect. When positions were reversed this difference became strikingly apparent to all.

Sr Agnes, in contrast to M. Teresa, was very gentle with me. Clearly she loved me with a love that was at first a delight and then a torment. Her love awoke a passionate, yearning 'crush' in my own starving heart. What I had feared and tried to avoid had happened. I was caught from the outset in the toils of an emotional involvement with the person responsible for my formation, with whom I must have continual and intimate contact. Carmel was no escape for me! Left to myself I would have escaped in many ways but God never let me. He was ruthless with me and needed to be. I could have no false ideas about myself. Oh, yes, I might pose a little before others as the budding contemplative and saint, but my heart had no illusions. I was made to see myself as I really am. The anguish of those early years is beyond recalling. I wonder how I endured. Pride, obstinacy, human respect, yes, undoubtedly, but I would suggest that these human factors only helped me to hold on to what in my deepest heart I knew was my treasure. I had seen, just for one brief moment, the dark door of vision, the mist-covered mountain summit, and I could never go back. The world had died for me. I could never go back to ordinary life. Were I to turn my back on Carmel I would be denying what had become part of me, had become my own reality. This emotional attachment was the first, overwhelming problem I had to face.

I needed no one to tell me that such a love as this was an obstacle. I felt it to be so. I was obsessed with it. It filled my thoughts. I experienced acute jealousy if I saw another novice receiving the attention for which I craved. And yet I had no doubt that I held supreme place in the mistress' heart. My sense of justice was offended when I saw her unfairly sharp with others while she would be all-loving to me. Homesick child that I was, I craved for her love and at the same time I experienced tearing guilt. I was ashamed of my involvement. I dreaded conferences or public reading lest anything be said about attachments and inordinate affections. I made pathetic efforts to withdraw from her. I knew she was just as involved as I and this made the situation infinitely worse. It was I who had to take the initiative in overcoming or modifying this involvement. She would not understand my crude efforts. I could not cope with the situation. More than once, alone in my cold, dark cell between compline and matins, my loneliness would overcome me and I would run to where she was next door. She welcomed me lovingly. She seemed the only warm thing in the desert which bruised me at every turn. At the back of my mind was the fear that the prioress would come to know of this attachment and how she would condemn it!

I could talk to no one of the difficulty, on the contrary I strove to conceal it. Looking back I would say that my instinct was correct. No one would have understood. Here things were black and white. One might have consoled me by telling me that 'of course we can love' whilst my heart would be telling me that this was not the sort of love that was meant. Another would have condemned it outright and only increased the sense of guilt. There was no one to show me the significance of the experience, the fundamental innocence of it and how to work through it into a mature relationship. But this, I am sure, was in God's plan. I was to learn by sheer experience the psychology of the human heart and how to lay it open to God. The suffering was worthwhile. I can understand others and their troubles in a deep way. I feel them from within and they realise it.

Introducing my superiors has led me off into this description of my emotional state; I must go back to more factual things. There was a certain charm in the atmosphere of the first few days. September can be beautiful and I spent some lovely hours with the novice—the only one at the time and a pleasant companion—picking apples or sweeping leaves. The scent of stored apples brings back the memory of those clear, clean days. Yes, there was a sense of clean austerity especially in my cell and bed and in the refectory. The poverty shocked me somewhat but at the same time I liked it. There was the pleasant sense too of being an interesting newcomer and I was well aware that I was looked upon with affection and approval. This I was never to doubt. It never entered my head that I might be sent away. I took it for granted that the decision rested with me. I was not long in perceiving, but not at that time consciously formulating, that I had a natural ascendancy in a community of simple people without great talent or personality. My youthful conceitedness judged them harshly. I was only a few months 'old' when I asked the mistress seriously if she considered this a real Carmel. Were they really nuns? This was a heartfelt question. I was not being impertinent or trying to be clever. I was concerned. Her answer did not reassure me but gave me a more sympathetic approach. Over and over again we novices were told that we were being given opportunities which had been denied the rest of the community. This could not reassure a very young person looking for guidance to the heights of the spiritual life! My mature judgment is that the faithful few who persevered were persons of real dedication with a spirit of devotion and sacrifice and most dear to God. They lacked training and were caught in the toils of a cramping system. They proved to be dear, loving, generous friends.

Soon the frosts came and cold weather set in. Then my penance began. I suffer from the cold. Not only does it affect me physically but it reduces me psychologically. There was no heating in the cold, damp house save a fire in the community room and in the novitiate oratory-cum-common-room. Day and night I was cold. I wondered how I would endure it. Others seemed to bear it so cheerfully while I felt utterly crushed. The following year some central heating was installed but, even so, cold was an extreme penance for me. I would go to bed cold and get up cold. I dreaded the long winter. Added to the cold was the darkness which depressed me. There was no electricity. Tiny gas flares cast a dim, bluish light on the staircases and passages. Each of us had a little oil lamp by which we could see to dress and undress. It was not much use for anything else. When darkness began to fall about four o'clock in late October and November, so did my spirits. A feeling of intense loneliness, fear, and unreality would enfold me. I would be working in the garden in the afternoons as the mist and darkness fell, digging up artichokes or weeding a rough part of the garden. This exercise was considered necessary for me. What a penance it was! It was the worms—great thick ones coiled round the sticky artichokes. I would suddenly find one sliding right by my foot, another against my hand or stuck on the end of my fork. I nearly screamed. I loathed them and could never get used to them. It was the practice to have a jar by one's side to collect them and throw them to the hens. I was unable to do this and awaited with dread the day when I would be ordered to pick up a worm. It never came.

Recreation was a little solace especially when the three of us could have it together in the novitiate. But I knew it would soon end and we would go off to the icy choir for compline. Then the hour alone in the dark, cold cell waiting the bell for matins. During my postulancy I would go to bed early several times a week. What a relief this was! When I was going to matins I was obliged to rest during this hour. Matins followed by lauds (this strange misplacement of lauds dates from the time of St Teresa) and a quarter of an hour's examen took us to about 10.40 when we retired, to rise at 5.40. How bitterly hard it was! The office was in latin and meaningless to me even though I could understand latin. I could not see how it could be a prayer, and I once said with some heat: 'I must just as well be rattling off nursery rhymes' and was sharply reproved. In summer time we rose at 4.40 but took an hour's siesta at midday. Although the lack of sleep was a big difficulty, still it was summer, and that fact compensated. It was the winter which was so bitterly hard. We fasted from September 14th until Easter and this aggravated the cold. From the time I was professed at nineteen, I was keeping the full regime save for an occasional early night. A hard regime indeed for a young girl lacking all interior comfort. The early years were little more than a test of endurance. It was impossible to give one's energies to anything but enduring. Thus I learned another lesson. Physical hardship, time-honoured standards of austerity, can be inimical to true growth in the spiritual life. Physical austerity must be carefully measured to capacity, it must be kept in its place, put wholly at the service of love, never allowed to replace love. I was utterly ashamed of my 'immortification'. I thought of St Thérèse's heroism in bearing much harder austerity than I and, well, just look at me!

In my early years in Carmel we were expected to eat a very big dinner, especially in the fasting season. The food, apart from the vegetables and fruit we grew ourselves, was of poor quality and markedly deficient in protein. We were too poor to buy milk. We relied on our poultry for eggs—no wonder worms were valued! Consequently it was considered necessary to eat large quantities of the food we had. My complicated self tied itself in knots in the refectory. I did not want to get fat and the diet was a fattening one. What is more, I had come to think it rather coarse to have a big appetite and eat a lot. I thought it rather unbecoming that nuns should eat so heartily. Also any book on the spiritual life one picked up spoke of the necessity of fasting. Our own *Rule and Constitutions* demanded it. Where then was the consistency? There seemed to me a lack of authenticity here, one of the many instances which I was to note, to fret over and finally work to resolve. My love of being singular and to excel prompted me along the path of abstention and above all, the craving for attention and sympathy. Not to eat was a way, a dishonest way, of stating that 'I am not well. I am suffering' With the prioress, M Teresa, there was no response save a sharp rebuke to eat what I was given.

Later on, when I was working harder, keeping the full timetable, and suffering from cold, food became an obsession. This difficulty was to last for many, many years. I found it extremely humiliating and tried never to let anyone see how bothered I was about food. I saw that others suffered from the same difficulty and I was determined I was not going to be alongside them. In later years, I have looked carefully at this phenomenon, which a wider experience

47

has shown to be quite common in our monasteries. The explanation seems to be that, in a life so deprived of comfort on every level, any little comfort offered is rabidly grasped. There are two sources of comfort, bed and food, and need for these can be tyrannical. Surely there must be something unbalanced in a regime which, far from freeing people, binds them to such animal needs. Experience has proved that when sisters are truly happy, are given adequate worthy interests wholly compatible with the contemplative life, such as good reading, interesting, creative, responsible work, and above all emotional satisfaction in human relationships, food and sleep cease to be important. They fall into the normal pattern. Preoccupation with food and sleep always leads me to suspect the supposed well-being of a given community. It is a symptom of a disease and should not be ignored or considered of little consequence.

My first letter from home arrived at the end of my first week, a fat envelope addressed in Betty's handwriting. Already I had grasped that, in Carmel, one's time is not one's own, 'it belongs to religion', that one lives strictly according to schedule with no free interludes in which one can relax and use as one pleases. Any spare few moments must be given to sewing which was always at hand in one's cell. So the precious letter would have to burn a hole in my pocket until the midday siesta or until after compline. However, our mistress met me and told me to open it. I took it to my cell and read it, or them, for there were several letters in one; chatty letters, telling me what was going on, full of slang and jokes, no moaning or wailing. Mother's letter was quiet and factual. She knew that letters were opened before being given to me and that my letters home were censored. Carefully I controlled my imagination. I shut off emotion and lived 'away' from my family. Possibly it was the only thing to do at the time. Later on, I cannot remember when, our mistress told me that I must have it out with myself. I did. I allowed the full flood of sorrow to sweep over me. I had lost them, my mother, father, my lovely, dear sisters and brother. Betty and Mary were particularly close to me. They would grow up without me. Gradually I would slip out of their lives and cease to be part of the family. Yes, they were truly, truly lost. Somehow or other I was able to grapple with this. I thought of eternity and that, if it was for God I cut myself from them, then

48

ultimately all would be well. In heaven I would be with them again. But heaven seemed to have little reality in my dark, bleak consciousness.

Mother and Daddy together with some members of the family would come to see me regularly. I looked forward intensely to their visit although another part of me told me it was foolish to do so. The visit would pass and I would be left in desolation. And so it was. I never gave my family the slightest suspicion of my unhappiness. I would watch out for signs to indicate whether the tension between my parents had abated at all. I began to think so. I had to wait until my veiling day, five years later, when for the first time Mother and I were alone for half an hour and she told me that things were ever so much better. Once, as the family were leaving the parlour, James came swiftly over to the grille and whispered: 'Mother and Daddy are much better, Ruddy'. Whilst I was a novice I was allowed to be alone in the parlour with my immediate family although our mistress often accompanied me. As it happened, my parents so liked her and she them, that the companion in the parlour was no hardship. In fact, I am sure they would have missed not seeing her.

However, the practice itself upset me greatly. After my first profession I was told that henceforth I could never go to the parlour alone, always someone must be with me. This disgusted me and I gave way to indignant anger and tears. I think this was justified. This form of mortification seems to me cruel to parents as well as to daughter. It was really saying: 'There is a gulf between you and us. We pay lip service to the fact that we love our families still and are concerned for them, but in reality we need to keep them at as great a distance as possible. They are in a different world from us.' It was surely enough that there was a small-meshed iron grille, as well as a wooden barred one separating us, allowing not the slightest physical contact, without depriving us of the intimacy of privacy. I shudder now when I think of what my mother must have suffered, she who loved her children with such a deep, passionate love.

Already there was present the same conflict there had been between school and home. All right, I had chosen to live in Carmel because God wanted it, but it was not home and never would be. It was no good anyone trying to suggest that I had in Carmel any substitute for my home. Carmel was hateful on the level that home was sweet. No one in Carmel could equal my mother and sisters. Only in the last few years have I brought myself to speak of my monastery as home. Home for me was my family. Always there was a sort of hostility for Carmel as though I had been put there against my will. I think it had a lot to do with the loss of independence, a feeling of insecurity because of this loss, a feeling of helplessness that I had no private life any more.

A postulant considerably older than myself entered a month or two later. She was of robin-like proportions and had a waspy tongue. I was told that she was a lay postulant. This puzzled me. Stefana, I knew was a qualified teacher, why should she be a lay sister? The decision seemed completely arbitrary. One of the three lay sisters was failing and another was needed. Stefana was physically strong. Later I learned that she had been in another Carmel but was not accepted for solemn profession. These circumstances undoubtedly affected her spirit. The situation was fraught with tension. Here was a younger person obviously more liked, quicker in every way. She must have felt jealous of me even though she was fond of me. She would cut me with her tongue. Her manner tended to be haughty and rude whereas I, thanks to my home and convent-school background, was considered kind and courteous. It was natural for me to be respectful to my elders. Poor Stefana found it hard going and I was sorry for her. However, the prioress clearly preferred her and chose to have her working with her. I had no envy of the privilege! Once when our mistress came to tell me, thinking it would be a pleasant surprise, that our mother wanted me to help her with some work, I nearly wept with dismay. I was afraid of M. Teresa's sharp tongue, afraid of all she stood for. If she represented the spirit of Carmel then I hated Carmel.

More than once I collapsed in tears under M. Teresa's sharp tongue. I was unbearably sensitive. It was the custom to ask leave to go from choir if one had a fit of noisy coughing. One night at matins during my postulancy, having a bad cold, I began to cough in a way I could not control and plucked up courage to go up to the prioress and ask if I might leave. She said in a scornful sort of way: 'You need to learn to blow your nose properly, that's all.' I went to my cell and burst into tears. I was angry, I was lonely, longing to be loved. Another time, at recreation, she snapped at me because I upset something or other. Again I could not hold back the tears, and failure to do so led to a hopeless fit of weeping. My instinct was to dash from the room but I knew I must not, that I must stay there and accept the misery and humiliation. The community were always sweet and non-condemnatory. The prioress merely shrugged her shoulders and said something about being a stupid baby.

Often M.Teresa would speak of our holy Mother Teresa as if she were in her confidence, quoting her sayings and anecdotes from her life. I tended to identify the two. What is more, I had delved into the *Way of Perfection* and had taken umbrage at St Teresa's attitude to women—so like our prioress' who had little respect for women. It was her boast that she had enjoyed the great advantage of being brought up with boys. This, we were told, had made the difference. Anyone could tell she had profited by male influence. My thoughts went to my fine mother and sisters. I was shocked by St Teresa's attitude to one's family as expounded in the *Way of Perfection*. She inveighed against attachments and had no patience with 'weepy wailies'. I feared St Teresa for I felt so far removed from her. At 28 I could moan from my heart to a confessor: 'I am sure St Teresa would never have accepted me'. 'She would have accepted you and made a fine nun of you', was his firm assurance.

The novice who was my first companion was sent away. It was done secretly and I was not told until she failed to appear at the next novitiate exercise. Later she married. One of the sisters in final vows left. This was a big shock. I was told it was due to continual infidelity. It sounded dreadful.

The strong feeling that there was no God accompanied me into the house of prayer. What an anomaly it seemed! After some time I told our mistress of it. I cannot remember what she said. At one of my rare interviews with the prioress I told her and she replied with her usual brusqueness: 'Of course there is a God'. This unhesitating assertion of an obvious fact helped me. But there was not the slightest gleam, not the slightest thought that made any impression on me or feeling that touched me. During the two hours of mental prayer which is part of our rule, the postulants and novices were in the middle of the choir facing the black shutter which was always across the opening looking on to the sanctuary. For mass, the shutter was drawn back but a thin veil covered the opening through which the priest and altar could vaguely be seen but, lest the nuns should be seen by the priest or servers, the choir was in stifling darkness. Prayertime was sheer tedium and I was only too glad when for some reason or other I was excused from it. My inner state frightened me. Something must be very wrong with me. I must not let any one know or else it will be thought I have no vocation to the contemplative life. I tried to make at least something happen to me that might sound convincing and interesting. There were one or two books in the novitiate on prayer. I read about the different stages—reading, reflection, affections and then the prayer of simplicity. Meditation and making of affections seemed quite impossible. Rather than admit that I had to begin at the beginning and be patient, I decided that I would opt for the prayer of simplicity, for a time impressing my mistress. I soon had to admit utter helplessness. Nevertheless, genuine, humble effort were of no avail and from that day to this how to pray has been an enormous problem. I have never been able to convince those whose help I have sought of the all-round realism of my problem. I felt no one has really grasped how total my inability was or is. From my earliest childhood God has hidden himself and hides himself still, but now I am happy that this is so.

The novitiate library was very impoverished. The community had not the money to buy many books but there was a keen desire to build up a library and we were told to ask for books when friends or relatives wished to make gifts. There was little that attracted me. I was afraid of books on the spiritual life for they made me feel so hopeless. Abbot Marmion's *Christ the Life of the Soul* was on the shelves and this appealed to me. It was objective. It did not talk about degrees in the spiritual life, it talked about Christ and our union with him. I found some comfort and support in this book. Likewise our mistress used to read a treatise on the *Precautions of St John of the Cross* by a Spanish Carmelite. This was not a frightening book. It was full of love and gentleness and, at the time, the only book on Carmelite spirituality that I liked. It helped me a great deal and, I would say, set a direction for me in the way of practising virtue. I was still very worried about the attachment to our mistress but, on the other hand, this writer spoke with such understanding that I felt less guilty. I learned not to concern myself with other people's business, to find a kind construction for their faults, to have a supernatural view of the Superior and other things besides. I am not saying I carried out these teachings but they sank into my mind and established a standard of conduct no matter how far I fell below it. It was a spirituality I could understand and want. It was true and full of love.

I took St Thérèse as my model of faithfulness in little things. I think this was all I had learned from her so far. In the novitiate we were taught a host of tiny practices regulating almost the whole of our conduct throughout the day: how to get up, how to make the bed, how to sweep the cell, how to eat in the refectory and so on. Once one had mastered these ways the mind could be occupied with God whilst one accomplished duties neatly and efficiently. We were also taught that, by the faithful observance of these details, we were certain of doing the will of God from morning until night. It seemed that holiness consisted in this. St Thérèse would seem to support this teaching and so I gave myself unquestioningly to it. Young, quick, with a good memory, I was soon adept. I am sure that I wanted to do this for the love of God but there was an enormous amount of self-love in it. It was an external sign of perfection, a way of being the perfect novice. Add to this the faithful observance of silence even when accosted by a senior, an outward docility, a willingness to help wherever I was needed and it is easy to see that I was considered a 'treasure' by some members of the community.

I looked around and saw that few were so faithful as I. Although I found a superficial satisfaction in this, my heart condemned me. I recognised the vanity, the lack of charity and meanness in regard to others. I was not deluded into thinking myself good even though it was a relief that others thought me so. Later I was to criticise severely this whole concept of 'observance'. Some people by tempperament are quite unable to pay attention to these minutiae. They are absent-minded, forgetful or lacking in observation and so outwardly may 'fail' much, and judged by the criterion of 'fidelity in observance' would be reckoned unfaithful, wanting in true obedience. I saw this happen. How false a view!

As far as I can remember my spiritual life consisted in little more than careful observance of all that was prescribed; trying to acquire the habit of the 'practice of the presence of God' as we were taught, offering each new duty to God before beginning it and making frequent 'acts' during work or when walking along the passages. I wanted to be a contemplative but seemed hopelessly removed from such a goal. All was utterly blank. For me God was not.

Is it possible to offer any explanation of this painful phenomenon? One that readily springs to mind is that it was a result of self-rejection; subconsciously I projected on to God my own sense of being utterly unlovable. In other words, there was an emotional block to all experience. This may be so but the fact that God was hidden from my very earliest childhood raises a doubt. The question could be asked, 'if some awareness of God's love had been there in childhood—most children seem to absorb this assurance naturally, given a loving home—would the self-rejection have been there, would it have grown? Rather, would not the sureness of being loved by God have counteracted it?' Another possible explanation for the bleakness of my early religious life would be simply lack of background. I knew so little about God so of course, coming to prayer, there was nothing to fall back on. There is, Ɩ think, a lot in this but, compared with many other postulants, I had an excellent background; brought up in a good catholic home and the practices common to such—prayers together, faithful church attendance. I had always attended a catholic school and received a thorough theoretical knowledge of doctrine at which I shone. Vim gave us a weekly conference which was, in fact, a spiritual talk and, I am sure, of a most helpful kind devotionally. It left me untouched. We had an annual retreat of three days. In the two years of sixth form Vim took us for a course of theology. All this remained 'outside' me. God, the object of it all, remained completely 'apart'.

I suggest that the sudden, powerful grace he gave me nullified, in a sense, all this theoretical knowledge. For many years I was to struggle with a subtle problem which now I can describe as that between God and the paraphernalia of God, if he will pardon me for

using the expression. There seemed no relation between God and all
that had been presented to me in teaching at school or what was
being offered to me in religious life. This conflict was to last for
many, many years, taking a somewhat different form. Now I realise
that, in a sense, it must always remain. In these early days teaching
was thin; apart from *Christ the Life of the Soul*, there was nothing to
impart real richness. I had not yet found Jesus and God in him. I
was lost, bewildered, with no helpful direction. No one understood
my problem. How could they? I could not express what I could not
bring to the surface of my own mind.

Fundamental to me is a natural fragility. My whole make-up
inevitably, I think, must experience void, peril, aloneness. Only an
extraordinary mystical grace could cancel these negative experiences,
and God has not chosen to give me this and I do not expect that he
ever will. He gave me one to 'start me off', to awaken me to seek for
him, to give my whole self to him, to show me that he alone was the
meaning of existence. For the rest, it is his will that I should grope
painfully along, experiencing to the depths what it is to be human, a
frail, human creature, belonging with all her fibres to this world yet
summoned beyond it, to a destiny bound up with the living God; a
child of earth called to be, dare I say it, the Son of God, for this is
what it means to be a christian, to be taken up into Jesus, to be identified with him, to become son in the Son; to enter the very family
life of the Trinity. 'He became poor that we might become rich.' I
was to experience the bare bones of human poverty.

Reading through what I have written on this period of my life, I
feel that I have not given an adequate impression of the dark shroud,
clammy and damp, which enveloped me continually. It was precisely
this which made everything else so hard to bear. It was always with
me. It felt like sin. It seemed sin, seemed to indicate that there was
no love for God in my heart. How was it compatible with love? Here
I was hating the life which was his choice and apparently so full of
him, utterly bored with prayer, finding not a scrap of satisfaction in
the divine office which, after all, was his praise. It was the same with
mass except that, thanks to help I had received from the priest who
directed me to Carmel, I had a few ideas which helped me to assist at
mass. And here was St Teresa saying that 'we make it our joy to

please God'. The prioress had sent me a card inscribed with this quotation before I entered. 'This place is a paradise for anyone whose sole aim is to please God' but hell for one not called to it. And there was young Thérèse and Elizabeth of the Trinity rhapsodising their joy at being in Carmel. As a postulant I confessed to being always depressed and sad. The confessor took up the point, saying there was no sin in this, rather it was a heavy cross laid on me so early in religious life. It would pass and God would give me consolation. This comforted me for a little while but I found it very hard to trust anyone sufficiently to accept his judgement.

Were there no pleasures in my young life? Very few. Simple festivities and relaxations at Christmas time and other rare occasions. I found myself throwing myself into these with intensity, only to find myself sick and weary afterwards. I remember looking forward to our mistress' feast. We had tea together in the novitiate and recreation for about an hour. It would be an occasion when I could embrace and kiss her without any feeling of illegitimacy. At a quarter to five, the clapper would go for preparation for prayer, silence would fall and depression even deeper would invade my poor heart. To avoid this intense feeling of sadness after such an occasion I learned to hold back from them, never to give myself wholly, to recall that they would soon pass, that only God was to be had and held in Carmel. 'Only you, my Jesus', is what my desolate, frozen heart has whispered a thousand, thousand times to him from my earliest days until now, but there was no answering response of love, no touch to reassure me that he was there, that he cared. I felt he cared nothing, that he had brought me into the desert to die of hunger and cold. I was utterly forlorn. As I said before, the love of our mistress was the only human comfort, but that was embittered with self-centred passion and consequent guilt feelings. He seemed to have let me down there also. Had I not tried to avoid this catastrophe? I smile at him now. 'My thoughts are not your thoughts, nor your thoughts my thoughts.' Quite so, Lord.

However this is not the whole truth. Whilst not wanting to minimise the well-nigh total absence of sense and emotional comfort, I must emphasise that, in a strange way, I was contented. Before I entered, I took it for granted that I would, from time to time, get a mad desire to escape and that it were better to keep away from the boundary wall. Walking round the garden was, apart from housework and gardening, the sole form of exercise, and we soon knew every blade of grass, every pebble of our small garden. A low wall, surmounted by a somewhat precarious fence which every now and then blew down, was our boundary. The road ran down one side and the other three sides were bordered with houses. Never did I feel the slightest wish to get out. Now and then I found myself reflecting that there was nothing I wanted. We had everything here . . . .and yet we had nothing! Perhaps a good way of expressing it is to say that I knew I was living. Oh, yes, it was painful but it was life, and the thought of life outside as I had known it and as, it seems, it was experienced by the majority of people, seemed hardly to be life. To look back would be comparable to an adult, in the midst of the difficulties of adult life, yearning for the carefree state of the unknowing child.

I was given the habit six months after my entrance. All the family came for the ceremony. I found some satisfaction in the little fuss and unusualness. Any break with routine was welcome. I had come to find a little relief even in using a different broom for a change! I made my profession of simple vows for three years in March the following year. The retreat of ten full days before profession is considered very sacred in Carmel. I was told that our mother would see me every day at four o'clock. This was a blow but I braced myself for whatever might transpire. The hour was spent in her telling me about the foundation of the house, scandals attached to it and other matters of Carmel. It was not serious giving of information. I felt it was little more than gossip and 'running down' of others. I had heard it done at recreation and I knew it was wrong. I had not the courage to say anything. I pretended to enter into it. I remember saying at the end, 'I am so glad to be in this Carmel'. These interviews—the tone and subject matter of them—upset me very much. In my puny way I had wanted to spend the retreat well but this information occupied my mind.

On the eve of my profession, whilst the community was at recreation in the evening, I went to a little summer-house in the garden. I remember standing there, looking at the house, looking at the fading sky. I had endured the ordeal of my second winter, spring was in the air, the garden patches around me were newly turned and raked, ready for the seed, there was a suspicion of swelling in the buds of the apple trees. Spring was before us. I had no illusions now. There was nothing whatever to look forward to humanly speaking. I was twenty years old and by all human standards an unhappy girl. Yet had I been asked what I wanted, was there anything I wanted, did anything 'outside' really pull me, I would have said 'No'. I had no God but nothing else could hold any real attraction for me. God had done his work thoroughly. 'Why, having wounded me have you fled away and left me to my groaning?' I would not have dreamed of applying these words of St John of the Cross to myself at this stage or even later. Such exalted language could never apply to the poor condition I was in. Only through teaching St John of the Cross to others, showing them the relevance of his teaching, have I come to apply the same to myself.

I have no clear recollection of my profession. It might not have happened for any repercussions on my emotional nature. Following the custom of Carmel I composed a song 'expressive of joy in their Profession and gratitude to God and the Community', and sang it at evening recreation. I chose the tune of Bach's chorale 'O Sacred Head'. There were, I think, only two verses. I cannot quote them but they were simply using the words of the mass, 'Accept, O Holy Father, this offering which we make to you'. I offered myself to the Father with Jesus and then brought the whole community into the second verse.

It was not a happy day, though, actress that I was, I concealed my feelings under gaiety. I have always thought of my solemn profession as my real profession. Perhaps God sees it differently.

5

GROANING IN TRAVAIL

A few months after my profession, the elections took place. They are held every three years in Carmel. It was St Teresa's wish that prioresses should hold office only for a short time. M. Teresa, through sheer necessity, had held the office of prioress for about twelve years, from the beginning of the foundation. It is not surprising, then, that a change of prioress should cause more than a ripple in the community. Sr Agnes was elected. This action of the community was a shock to M. Teresa who had not foreseen it. The change of prioress was momentous for the future of the Carmel and for me, and in order to bring this out fully I must pause to say something of the role and influence of a Carmelite prioress.

St Teresa wished the prioress to be a humble figure, in no way the 'grande dame', as were the abbesses of her time. She was to be given no title other than Mother Prioress; was to share in the chores of the house and, once out of office, was to return to her normal place in community. However, St Teresa exacted of her daughters a very great obedience to the prioress and counselled them to seek spiritual direction from her. No doubt in the early beginnings this was feasible enough. The prioress would be a well-trained nun capable of helping the newcomers. It is doubtful if St Teresa had in mind any other situation than that of the training period. As the order passed into royalist France, Netherlands, and Italy inevitably the image of the prioress changed somewhat. There was the tendency to surround her with honours and attentions. She tended to become the 'grande dame' in spite of contrary affirmations. If, through force of circumstances or otherwise, the one person held the office for a considerable time, then she became something of an absolute monarch.

M. Teresa in no way played the fine lady; she scrubbed many a floor and cleaned many a toilet. Nevertheless her rule was absolute. The enclosure of Carmel was rigid. Contact with the outside was minimal and under the complete control of the prioress. Nothing and no one could come in or go out without her knowledge. It was this severe form of enclosure which, in practice, ensured her total power and control of the sisters. She controlled their minds. No literature and hence no new idea or thought could get in. She alone was informed of what was going on outside and it rested with her whether information was passed on. She could and did keep the community in a state of ignorance. She could, and usually did, exercise the same restrictive role within the community itself. Sisters had practically no relations with one another. No one could speak intimately to another without asking leave from the prioress, and though St Teresa clearly made provision for this need in her constitutions, it was completely overlooked. No one thought of asking this permission. Only to the prioress could one speak of one's personal concerns. The recreation periods were formal. The prioress and subprioress sat at the top of the room, the rest of the community in two rows down each side, the lay sisters always at the bottom. The novitiate, when present at the community recreation, sat with their mistress next to the prioress. Endless were the topics forbidden at recreation. Anything personal, anything about one's family affairs was banned. Often it was difficult to find anything interesting to talk about. It was quite usual for the prioress to do the talking.

It is not surprising that, in such conditions, there was no one to replace the prioress and so she would continue in office and the evil of immaturity would be perpetuated. Our mother's word was absolute. It was sufficient to say: 'Our mother says...' in order to get an immediate response. It seems she knew everything. I remember questioning some point of history that was being discussed. I thought it was inaccurate, in fact was quite sure it was. My jaw dropped when one of the sisters said with an air of finality: 'It is true. Our mother says so.' I was a postulant at the time. There was only one will in the community and tended to be only one mind. It needed very great independence of mind and real enlightenment to preserve one's own truth. One of the most important matters taught was that our mother held the place of God. We must not question her orders. It was not only sisters who entered young who were reduced to mental immobility by this teaching. Women of mature age and great experience would accept this principle without question and see in it the supreme way of 'dying to self'. There is no doubt that it was the occasion of multiple acts of heroism on the part of a multitude of Carmelites. In earlier times it might be condoned but anyone who has experienced the harmful effects of this system must cry out against it.

Many injustices could be committed by the prioress and there would be no redress for the victim. The fascination of her office was such that most of the community would automatically be in sympathy with the prioress and automatically condemn the victim. I noticed that, if the prioress had her knife into a person, that sister became something of an outcast in the community, and often enough the 'unfaithful' 'disobedient' nun, the nun 'lacking in religious spirit and humility' was merely a potentially independent spirit who dared to question the prioress or show some frustration, temper and resentment. Rarely was any of this sort of thing done in malice. Usually the prioresses were kind women sincerely seeking what they thought to be the good of the sisters. But they lacked training, lacked a knowledge of themselves and so acted through emotional compulsions, obvious to others but hidden from themselves. Insecure in their position, basically afraid, the only way to govern successfully was by this way of supression. They could not afford to have independent people around them. Life would be too complicated; government extremely difficult. It was essential to maintain the mother-child role; the one who knows and the one who doesn't. There was little or no thought-out policy. One prioress would follow in the steps of another, conforming more or less to the same pattern. 'This has always been done', 'this has been the custom', were catchwords and not to be challenged.

Although visitations were carried out, rarely was the Visitor given any information detrimental to the prioress. I have known more than one situation where there were serious troubles in the community and, although the community was blessed with an excellent ecclesiastical superior who visited them frequently, not a word of it was said to him. The instinct of loyalty is very strong in a woman's community but the chief silencing factor springs from the power of the group or the one who is the heart and centre of the group. Even though sisters are well informed and know they have an absolute right and duty to speak to higher superiors of any thing that is wrong, nevertheless the influence and sanction of the prioress is experienced as stronger than that of a superior who, though 'higher', is not in the family circle. I think outside authority is not sufficiently aware of this. If a sister were to make some statement to the Visitor, unless she is tough or strongminded, she would feel she had betrayed the prioress, would find it difficult to look her in the face, to feel still a part of the community. These unhappy feelings could easily lead her to admit that she had spoken. Rather than undergo these psychological pressures, sisters decide not to speak. One has to live within an enclosed group really to understand the subtle dynamics which govern relationships within it.

It was a great relief to me, this change of office. Now it would be my dear Sr Agnes who would set the standard for the house, whose judgements would prevail. Her spirit, not that of M. Teresa, would be supreme. Trying to analyse why I was gratified that this was so, I would say that the chief reason was M. Teresa's inability really to love. She was kind and caring and fond of people, but I simply could not imagine her involved in another person, knowing the anguish of a great love, feeling that one's whole welfare hung on another. Her capacities were very limited, her range of interests, her pleasures, likes and dislikes on a small scale. With her everything was 'little': her conversation at recreation and in private, her occupations were of the simplest kind, and in them she found all she needed. Instinctively I was realising that she and I were in almost different worlds; that she would never understand me, never meet my requirements, and so I experienced a deep-down insecurity that was not merely a fear of being roughly treated, but a fear that I could never meet her requirements, never be the sort of Carmelite she had in mind and which was supposed to conform to St Teresa's ideal. Hence I was not a true Carmelite and the sense of guilt and failure haunted me. Now that was all changed. At the head of the house was a woman who really loved me, who would break her heart if I left, a woman who approved of me, valued me, who, though never understanding me,

seemed to recognise my potential. And, more objectively, I thought
M. Agnes far more virtuous than M. Teresa, who seemed to me
downright immortified although, whilst she was prioress, I never allowed myself deliberately to think so. M. Agnes was the perfectly
observant religious. I wanted my monastery to be fervent—I leave it
to God to weigh up why I wanted it fervent, otherwise I would go
dizzy with such complexity!

Although, inevitably, M. Teresa was appointed novice mistress
and therefore became my immediate superior, I preferred the
arrangement this way round for the reasons given. However, the
prospect before me was not a sunlit one. Yet it was not without its
light. I made up my mind to accept her and to show her the same
attention and give her the same trust as I had given to M. Agnes. My
attention, my trust, were not appreciated and I received many a curt
rebuff. She did not mean to be unkind, it was just that her manner
was discourteous and she disliked fuss. Of course she was sore at
the result of the election and her first words on taking up her job in
the novitiate were to the effect that she had had enough of looking
after people and would like a rest. M. Agnes had made no secret of
the fact that she loved her role of looking after her charges in the
novitiate. What a difference!

Sometime before these elections another postulant, Isabel, had
joined our novitiate, a beautiful woman a few years older than
myself, and she was like a big sister to me. Understandably she was
treated more gently by our mistress, but Stefana and I—I especially
—had been spoiled and now needed stern handling. I could not
please our mistress and yet I persevered in my intention of accepting
her as such. I plucked up courage to ask her for spiritual help. She
agreed to see me but clearly it was tiresome for her. We got nowhere.
On the other hand, she helped me by forcing me to control my tears,
to keep a stiff upper lip, and now and then made a kind remark as
she saw me struggling not to give way. In some ways this situation
was made easier by the fact that M. Agnes was in the background.
However, I realised that I must not escape from the painful effects of
M. Teresa's reprimands by flying to her. I made up my mind to
accept them and always to ponder what she said by way of criticism
to see if there was any truth in it. This is a habit I formed early in my

religious life and it has served me well. I never brush aside criticism. I always look for the truth in it. I am sure M. Teresa was good for me even though I found it hard to think that her treatment was not to some extent a result of her own hurt self-esteem. I may have been wrong. She was incapable of giving instruction or guidance as her own background and reading were so limited.

Eagerly I would look forward to a visit to M. Agnes, but again there was a fly in the ointment. I felt that M. Teresa disapproved although she could say nothing for I had every right to go to the prioress. The latter added to my unease by keeping me over the appointed time which would call the mistress' attention to the fact that I was with her. The prioress took no notice of my fidgets. Once in office she showed an amazing disregard of opinion. She pursued the course she thought right regardless of anyone's opinion or criticism. At the time I admired her for this singlemindedness; later I was to be more reserved. Was there not lack of regard for others' feelings and reactions? It was, or tended to be, a pursuit of duty, a steam roller of duty. Persons could be mown down and left by the wayside bleeding.

About this time we had a minor epidemic of flu, and because of the severe cold the prioress insisted that, once I was out of bed, I should go and sit in her room where a fire had been lit. She too was recovering from the flu. This was most embarassing for me. I was always there when anyone came to see her. One day M. Teresa exclaimed: 'Leave that novice alone. Let her learn to become a Carmelite'. Gladly would I have stayed in my cold cell rather than suffer this criticism, but M. Agnes brushed it aside and insisted I should be in the warmth.

Oh, how easy it is to throw out such glib remarks! I do not think anyone who has not personal experience of these emotional attachments or the dreadful emotional suffering involved in some psychological flaws can possibly understand them. So often have I heard the words, addressed to myself and others: 'You must overcome this attachment. You cannot give yourself to God whilst you are involved like this. Go to God. Pray. You will find all you need in God. God is all...' I have heard others say that their heart is free, they have found everything in God. How we can deceive ourselves! How I suspect glib assertions and edifying clichés. True freedom of heart is a pure gift of God. A person in possession of this freedom is full of compassion. Her heart is sensitive, quick to perceive the anguish of another, slow to deal in clichés. Usually this gift is not given except after much suffering. What often passes for freedom is lack of sensitivity or the indifference which is the result of repressed emotions. My own experience of myself and others has taught me that the only answer to these emotional sufferings is an understanding of suffering, a grasp that all these pains are a share in the cross of Christ. It is simply not true to say 'going to God', 'fidelity in prayer, etc', cure these wounds or break these attachments. These latter are on the emotional not the spiritual level. Prayer is not magic. God does not work miracles. Sometimes it is necessary to seek proper psychiatric help.

The fact is that women who in secular life would appear quite well-balanced, thrown into the desert of Carmel reveal their flaws. This is good. This is as it should be. Everything depends on this process being understood and exploited. The only answer to these emotional sufferings is acceptance until God ordains otherwise. They should be seen as opportunities for growth in love, for an increase in capacity. No one should be allowed to feel that she is guilty for these feelings. The suffering is cruel enough without adding the further one of guilt. The positive value of the experience must be pointed out and every encouragement given to bear this suffering in union with our Lord. The cross of Christ. This is its significance. It does not mean that something has gone wrong, that I am in the wrong place, that because my life is so suffering it must mean that God does not want me in this particular way of life. In fact, real insight is needed to discern when this 'unhappiness', these emotional sufferings, are indications of no vocation. The genuine vocation will respond to the sort of approach I have indicated.

After a year M. Teresa asked to be relieved of her charge of the novitiate. It was clear that bitterness was growing. There were signs of friction between her and the prioress. M. Teresa, because of her long term in office and because she had received and 'reared' most of the community, still enjoyed great prestige. It is amazing how blind women can be in their loyalty. To a newcomer she had glaring faults;

her 'daughters' seemed oblivious of them. A painful crisis was looming.

M. Agnes had no alternative but to appoint someone else as novice mistress and chose quite a young nun whom I felt was not sufficiently 'above' us to hold such an office. I felt a violent rebellion against this. Why such a revolt? I am sure my two companions experienced no such difficulty. I found the whole concept of the novitiate galling. We were reduced to the level of children, completely subservient and, so to speak, at the mercy of the superior. As I have pointed out earlier, I find subjection extremely difficult. It seems to hit at human dignity. It always grates. This complex of mine led me to examine the whole concept of authority and obedience. I would say that my attitude—blind, inexplicable though it seemed—was fundamentally healthy. There was no natural subservience in me even though I longed to please, longed to be liked and loved.

What is more, age-old traditions of kissing the floor and performing other gestures of humility and subjection were very much in vogue. At the slightest hint of reprimand one had to kiss the floor and remain in the state of prostration until told to rise. Each morning, at the novitiate exercise, the novices confessed their exterior faults or had them pointed out by the mistress. Once a week novitiate chapter was held. All these practices cost me a great deal. I tried to accept and fulfil them for God but I never overcame the revolt. Whilst M. Agnes was mistress, or even M. Teresa, because she was so used to it all and we sensed it was nothing but routine to her, it was more possible to cope with, but the thought of bringing another into the scene of our humiliating performance was just too much. I fell into a rage and declared I would never, never accept and, indeed, I felt that I *could* not accept. It was in this and other similar seemingly insuperable difficulties, when my whole being was in revolt, that I learned the power of God. I am faced too with the mystery of human choice. In the midst of this turmoil, when everything in me was raging 'can't, can't', some fine point sought for God's hand. I seemed able, not to overcome the conflict, not to emerge from the storm but, in the very midst of the storm, engulfed in the 'can't' as it were, to move forward to God, leaving it to him to enable me to do what I experienced as impossible.

This was a striking example. I went to choir, just showed my heart and told him I could not want to give in unless he gave me the preliminary grace. He did. Peace came. I resolved to accept wholeheartedly and to give the new mistress (who seemed to me sluggish and dull) all the respect and rights which were due to her. I remember her making the remark that it would be nice to have a spray of roses before the statue of our Lady in the novitiate. At the first opportunity I went out and cut one. Others, I was well aware, considered this sort of thing as currying favour.

I expected nothing for my twenty-first birthday and was touched at the little celebrations prepared for me in the novitiate by Isabel and Stefana. They were truly fond of me and on my side I tried to make up for the difficulty of the situation. We novices made the crib at Christmas. I liked this sort of thing and would come up with bright ideas. Deliberately I gave Stefana full say and accepted the office of apprentice. In her absorption in the task she would become sharp and bossy. On the first occasion we made the crib together, both of us had worn ourselves out, scratched one another and so approached the Christmas feast feeling rather smutty. It was the same the following years but I was able to offer my feelings of failure to our Lord, vaguely understanding that this would please him more than if everything had gone swimmingly and I had emerged with flying colours. All three of us liked dramatics and would get up performances for the community. Again there were clashes but again I learned to give in to Stefana. I must say I felt some superiority when she gave way to temper, stalked out of the novitiate in a rage, left her duties undone and was in open revolt. I never did such things. I was soon to see clearly in a humiliating way that I lacked the courage and honesty for this open show. I resorted to covert means.

Tension in the community was mounting. In particular there was one thoroughly neurotic sister who caused the prioress a great deal of anxiety. She and M. Teresa, possibly because they were near in age, tended to sympathise with one another. This Sr Patricia had a way of getting at the prioress through us novices who, it was thought, were the apple of her eye.

There was indeed the tendency for M. Agnes to regard us as rather precious. We were her product, we embodied her teaching and training. One day at chapter, when, as usual, the chapter nuns were asked if they had anything to say about the sisters of the novitiate, kneeling in the middle of the room, Sr Patricia made some slight observation. It was unjust in itself and what is more, I felt quite sure she was saying it out of malice. The prioress reproved me. In itself it was a mere nothing but I was overwhelmed by the sense of lovelessness, my sensitivity was wounded to the quick and I began to cry. The barrier once down there was no stopping the flood of tears. I felt utterly humiliated. When we left the chapter room whilst the seniors confessed their faults I was still weeping, and weeping when we returned, summoned by the bell. From the chapter room we proceeded in procession to the refectory for evening collation, juniors leading. The lay sisters, who had left the chapter room before the choir nuns of simple profession acknowledged their faults, were waiting in the refectory. I knew I would be the object of their curious speculation. I felt I had had enough. I could not go to the refectory. I dropped out of rank and the procession passed on without me. The situation was even worse now. The prioress, passing last, whispered: 'Sister, come to the refectory'. In a moment of time I was faced with a choice. I knew it to be momentous. I seemed to realise that, if I refused, if I disobeyed, it would be the beginning of the end for me. I followed on, behind the prioress and thus, more conspicuous than ever, still weeping. I went to recreation as usual. M. Agnes sent me to bed after compline. I sat on the edge of my bed in utter misery and helplessness. There was a gentle tap and the infirmarian came in with a cup of ovaltine. I was touched, but so hated myself that I found it hard to accept this act of kindness. Her face was gentle with sympathy. When the community returned from Matins I was still sitting on the bed immersed in gloom. I was back again in the old moods of bygone days and I was utterly discouraged. The door opened softly and M. Agnes came in. She took me in her arms and comforted me. She settled me in bed with a mother's love.

I must say something about my hatred of chapter. During my year as an unprofessed novice I endured it as one of those hard things to be expected in religious life. The fact that M. Teresa presided made it easier to bear. She was no mother, anyway. Also, she, as far as I remember, never reproved me in chapter. But when M. Agnes as prioress presided, then the incongruity of it struck me with full force. The prioress was supposed to be a mother; St Teresa expressly said so. The community was a family. Love was the predominant note. Where then did these strange proceedings fit it? The 'mother' sat in the chair of office, delivered a conference and then the correction of faults began. It was the prioress' job to reprove and give penances. It was not that anything terrible ever happened, it was just that it offended all my sense of 'mother', 'sisters', 'home'. It made Carmel seem bleaker than ever, a house of correction and, indeed, only too easily could it assume this atmosphere. With all my being I resented it; resented the humiliating position it put me in. This conflict reached such proportions that, before the chapter, I would lie flat on the floor of my cell in real pain, begging for the grace to accept. Accept I did.

I had a similar bitter conflict over the discipline when first introduced to it. 'Never', I said, 'I can't'. Again I got the grace to accept. But I could never reconcile myself to these practices as such. Later on, as I shall tell, I was to think through this problem of 'artificial' penance and reach my own conclusions. At this time I rejected them as valuable or even right in themselves, but accepted them because it seemed right to accept them at the present moment.

I have mentioned earlier that the night office was extremely onerous for me especially in the winter time. I used to long for the word sending me to bed early. This usually came during a period. It was the custom to rise an hour later for three mornings at a period, thus everyone knew that it was on. Normally the prioress or mistress would tell the sister to miss matins one night also. My periods were very irregular. Sometimes six weeks, sometimes eight, and thus I felt myself rather badly done to. I found myself crawling to matins with a shrinking reluctant spirit. We had the devotion of renewing our vows each year. We were recommended to make it an occasion for forming some resolution. I entered into this ceremony as wholeheartedly as I could and made a point of offering something to God. On one of these occasions I offered God the night office. I offered it in all its repugnance. From then on I was able to accept it fully and thus it lost some of its grimness. I was trying in all the ways I could, to do what I ought, to accept, to bow my stubborn neck. I formed habits of always answering bells promptly no matter how interesting the work I was doing or the book I was reading: I tried to restrain my curiosity and keep control of my eyes.

Shortly after the appointment of the new mistress I had my first fit of hysterics. It was in the middle of the summer. No doubt I was physically exhausted and my nerves were at breaking point. All the same, the hysterics were the outward expression of acute jealousy and frustration. The postulant had an abscess or something and was getting a lot of attention from M. Agnes. One day we were in the novitiate and I heard a murmur of voices. I knew that M. Agnes was in the postulant's cell which was off the novitiate. Suddenly my self-control snapped. I sprang up and beat on the door with my fists. Startled, the prioress opened the door to be met by my fury. I gave way completely, letting my body have full play, letting it contort. I was fully conscious. Those present shook me and slapped me and eventually brought me back to sanity. I was seized by a dreadful sense of shame. I think it occurred once or perhaps twice more in this acute form and a few more times in a milder way. Always M. Agnes was involved. These attacks left me with a permanent sense of shame the more so as they were kindly interpreted. No one attributed them to furious jealousy, to raging anger, which is what they were. Years later, I discussed the matter with an experienced priest. I said I was incapable of forming a judgment as to my culpability. He agreed this was impossible and that it did not matter. He made light of the affair, declaring that in all probability I was saved from a nervous breakdown in this way. Certainly I remember that, in spite of the humiliation, an attack was followed by a great sense of release and calm. Possibly it was a way of releasing all my nerves, rather in the same way as giving oneself up to a tortuous, self-expressive dance. At the time I could not judge it so lightly. I felt a hypocrite. I was shamed to the roots of my being.

In the early summer of 1950, M. Agnes had to go to hospital for surgery. She was away for a month. As the subprioress was a young woman and of delicate health—she had been ill herself—M. Agnes appointed M. Teresa as vicaress. I was appalled and soon my fears, which no one else seemed to share, were justified. She used her authority to undermine that of the prioress, speaking freely of the changed spirit in the house. Her influence was great since the majority of the community had been with her for many years, whereas M. Agnes was, comparatively, a newcomer. I felt the changed atmosphere, knew so much was in peril, and I was helpless. To begin with I was seized with irrational fear that M. Agnes would die or be incapable of continuing in the office of prioress. What is more, I missed her. There could be no communication. In spite of all my efforts, when I realised the prospect before us of weeks without her, the tears forced their way through. These were perceived by the novice mistress. She called me to her and, free from the inhibitions and restraining influence that M. Agnes' presence in the house would have caused, spoke her mind. The sum of it all was that she thought I should leave Carmel. I had already given evidence that it was beyond my nervous and emotional strength. I ought to go before it was too late. Obviously she was in a state of great agitation and went on to tell me that she intended to leave and had written for a dispensation from her vows. She described how she had left everything to enter Carmel: her career, the man she loved, and had been completely disillusioned. God was not in our Carmels. Our particular Carmel was founded against God's will. His grace was not with us. The community seethed with disunity and unrest. With the election of M. Agnes she had hoped for better things, but as things were, she was convinced there was no point in staying.

Although I was utterly astounded and shaken by these words, I felt strangely calm and grown-up. It was as if I realised I was being put to the test in a big way. More was to come. M. Teresa sent for me and she too pointed out that I was not suited to the life, for I was far too highly-strung and if I had bent so under my little troubles, what about the greater ones which would be sure to come? I stood my ground saying that, all the same, I was sure my vocation lay in Carmel. If I had had reason to respect her judgment I might have been influenced, but as it was, although I was under her immediate influence and therefore, insecure as I was, impressed and shaken, I knew M. Agnes had a different opinion. M. Teresa went on to complain how the spirit of the house had changed, that M. Agnes was not obeying the constitutions. When I asked her on which points, she could not answer specifically , but only that every point could be kept and yet the spirit be all wrong.

I left her reeling. There was no one I could turn to. I had to bear the weight of it alone. When I was free I went down into the garden. There was a high wind and so I could cry aloud without being heard. I cried out to God, cried out in pain, asking him to take the chalice away. My world had fallen to pieces. As regards the house, all my hopes were centred on M. Agnes. With her at the head, we could become a true Carmel. But was it so? Was M. Teresa right? Were there things happening of which I knew nothing? And then, for the first time, I realised my vocation was in question. Were M. Teresa and the mistress right? I had also to face the fact that, were M. Teresa to return to office before my solemn profession, it might well never take place.

I would sit in my cell during those awful weeks, wondering what was happening in the community which was vibrant with tensions. I found myself repeating with deep feeling a chapter from the *Imitation of Christ:* 'O just Father . . .the hour has come for your servant to be tried . . . the hour thou foresawest from all eternity. That Thy servant for a short time should be oppressed without but always live to Thee; that she should be a little slighted and humbled and fail in the sight of men . . . so that she may rise again . . .it is good that shame hath covered my face . .' Yes, I was beginning to find meaning in it, to find God hidden in the depths of my poverty.

At last I wrote to the priest who had guided me—the friend of my mother. I had to ask M. Teresa's permission for this, which she kindly gave. I told him of all that had happened and asked what he thought. He took some time to reply but his answer was reassuring. He put things into perspective for me, pointing out the inexcusable, unambiguous folly of the two officials. Moreover, he reaffirmed his belief in my vocation, saying it stood out clearly from the pages of my letter.

One evening during this time, my eyes fell on the words: 'O the depths of the riches and wisdom of God! How incomprehensible his judgements, how unsearchable his ways!' In the depths of my soul I became aware of a steadfast peace. The world could rock and reel. Everything and everyone could fail me. I myself could be broken, could be a complete failure in the eyes of men but nothing could prevent me from loving God. I was faced with the possible breakup of the Carmel or my own rejection by the community. But nothing could prevent me from giving myself to God. I remember distinctly it was this way round. It was still impossible to make real to myself in any way that God loved me even though I made continual acts of faith and tried to act as if I were sure of his love.

It seems to me that God has given me the grace to seek the truth and to stand in the truth, and essentially this means the truth about myself. I may be very blind and thus speaking in blindness but, as far as I can see, a steady light always shone in my heart which revealed me to myself, whatever impression might be given outwardly. I think, too, I accepted this light and opened myself to it. I have already mentioned that I would take to heart whatever was said by way of criticism—too much to heart. Early in my spiritual life I was given a deep self-knowledge. This was to be the foundation on which God wished to build. It forced me into the arms of his mercy. At the end of her life St Thérèse declared that she 'had understood humility of heart'. Here I am daring to say that I too have understood humility of heart. I do not say that I am humble of heart but I understand that the principal work of God is to bring us to true humility and poverty of spirit, to make us deeply aware of our nothingness so that he can give himself to us. Everything depends on our willingness to stand in the truth, to refuse to escape from this painful revelation of self, to accept to stand naked before the living God. At this time I was far from grounded in trust, that trust which casts itself into the arms of God, but I was growing towards it. After a fall, after some revelation of my weakness, feeling utterly wretched, when my instinct was to sulk spiritually, or at least be sluggish (through disgust with myself) in returning to God with full heart, recalling the story of the prodigal and that the father had embraced him in his smelly rags and that it was the father who cleansed and adorned him, I would say to him: 'I ask you to love me all the more, to do more and more for me just because I have failed'. This quiet inward working, this gentle turning to God in rain, fog, sleet has gone on unremittingly. Although I might express in words bitterness, despair, utter frustration, my heart spoke lovingly to God. Often I would be gripped in emotional rebellion and resentment—but my heart would lie in suffering acceptance at God's feet.

Another precious grace of God was the realisation of the supreme importance of charity. I grasped that this was the real proof of love for God; was, indeed, the way in which we loved God—the only way—and I set about it in earnest. As soon as one determines on this course it appears as endless and of infinite ramifications. More and more I am given to see how self-love masquerades under love of the neighbour; how what appears to be the pure love and service of others is riddled with selfish motives. At one time I used to be distressed by this impurity of motive which I detected in all my thoughts and actions; now I no longer expect or claim that anything I do is purely for God. I want it to be so and try for purity of heart but am content to see the smears of self. Only he can bring about total purity, perfect love. Nowhere so much as in the practice of charity was I made so aware of my sinfulness, my selfishness. I would pray God to create a clean heart in me, to take the stony heart out of my breast and give me a heart of flesh. Perceptive, quick to see the flaws in another, I was prone to criticism, finding a certain satisfaction in seeing another at fault as though this, in some way, raised me up. I knew that no fault would so displease our Lord or stop his grace as this harsh judgement on his children. I realised I had the mentality of a pharisee but, I thought to myself, if a pharisee had turned to our Lord and admitted his hardness of heart, his crabbed, mean spirit and asked for help, our Lord would have helped him. So I did the same. The pharisee became the publican. I came to realise that temptations to pride, the sins of the pharisee, could make one a publican. The stone which the builders rejected could become head of the corner. I tried to use these bad tendencies to grow in humility. I realised charity must be in the heart and so tried to think kindly and lovingly.

I have made it a principle always to put others first; to think what would be best for others, to prefer their convenience to my own. This is my aim; I am not always faithful to it. I am not naturally loving. I am kindhearted when it does not cost much but am far too egocentric to love easily. I have had to fight every inch of the way in order to love others.

In true love for our neighbour lies all the asceticism we need. Here is the way we die to self. What are disciplines, artificial practices of penance and humility compared with this relentless pursuit of love? Perfect love of the neighbour means complete death to self and the triumph of the life of Jesus in us.

6

YET WILL I TRUST

I find it hard to give a clear picture of my life, because of its complexity, but if it is of moment to our Lord that a true picture should emerge, then I am confident that he will help me. It is not possible to be completely accurate in the time sequence; to say with certainty that at this particular point it was like this and then it changed to that, any more than one could report with absolute chronological accuracy the changing sweep of the sky or a landscape on a fitful day. I inevitably run ahead and find myself speaking of later developments, but human life is a whole, it is fluid and difficult to lay hold on. And it seems to me that my life, in particular, is a whole. No great gulf seems to separate me from the child, girl, the young nun. I seem to have the same difficulties, the same tendencies. It seems to me, looking back on my early religious life, that already all the essentials were there, the insights and general orientation, so that significant inaccuracy is almost impossible.

I discovered the gospels. In the fifth and sixth forms at school we had studied Matthew and Luke. I had found great beauty in the latter but, as far as awareness goes, it made no personal impact. Shortly before I entered I had looked at John. It seemed obscure and difficult but, nevertheless, held a fascination for me. I can say now that the gospel of John has been my bread of life, the ground of my faith and the rock to which I clung in constant doubts against faith. I read with awe the mysterious prologue and then the beautiful scenes of the apostles' call. 'Master, where do you live?' I pondered long and lovingly on the texts and my keen mind and imagination were at work. I read the other gospels but none appealed as this one. There was something unassailable about it. The Jesus that got across, the words he uttered, carried their own credentials. 'This is no purely human document.' That impression, that conviction, has

77

never faded. I loved too the infancy narratives of Luke. I found the birth, infancy and childhood of Christ easy to dwell on. I think this was due to the fact that here one faced the mystery of the incarnation starkly. 'The Word was made flesh'—in this mute, almost formless baby. There was no need to form a picture. Whereas, when I wanted to think of the man Christ, I was faced with a difficulty. The pictures which had been presented to me over my life were off-putting and yet I could not free myself from these images when I wanted to think of him. How I welcomed an occasional glimpse of what he might have looked like as a boy or man and this was more likely to be in a real photograph of an Arab boy or swarthy Indian. I found it helpful to look at pictures: a mother with a baby . . . my thoughts would wander over it . . .the helplessness, the relationship between them, breast-feeding . . . his need of her . . . and then 'this is God'. Here began, here were laid the foundations of my absorption in the mystery of the incarnation. In the study of the childhood and hidden life of our Lord and our Lady, I came to see the significance of the contemplative life which was a great help to me. Also I had a faded picture of our Lord calming the storm at sea. Its fadedness was a help for no features were seen, it was more suggestive than vivid and it left my thoughts free to go beyond to the person.

Having described what seems to be an era of light and consolation I have immediately to cancel it out and cry: 'No, no, there was no consolation'. How explain this contradiction which has persisted most of my life. Round about the time of my final vows I discovered Ephesians. My mind sank into it but I am sure it was no merely speculative study. It was contemplative. I found myself abounding in lights and would gladly discuss them with others if I got the chance at recreation. I began to well up like a fountain and others caught the falling spray. This has never ceased though there have been times of greater and lesser abundance. When people have told me of aridity in prayer and I have replied by saying that I know it too, they have laughed at me: 'You, arid in prayer, with all your lovely thoughts!' The fact is that I can never hope to show how, in some mysterious way, I myself was shut off from this world of light and beauty.

Was it that the deep sense of sinfulness, the dreadful image of myself, cut me off? It is possible, but considering that I dwelt long and lovingly on the story of the prodigal and used and still use this exquisite thing to show: 'Look, this is the true God, this is his attitude to you' and, in that part of me which I could control, applied it to myself and established myself in trust upon it, I think we cannot say that this is the sole explanation.

I am inclined to think the explanation lies along these lines: as I have pointed out when speaking of my girlhood, my whole being seems poised to leap towards another person. Ideas, things, cannot really touch me. They occupy and amuse me a little but fail to touch *me*. This 'me' is experienced as an incompleteness, as a half-thing meaningless in itself and bleeding, moaning, groaning, tormented until it finds its other self, until it is united to another person. Here, undoubtedly, is a strong sexuality. This human need which, in God's plan, is normally orientated to marriage, the symbol-fulfilment, in its profoundest reality is a need for God and, in my own case, this was experienced without mitigation. The sheer exposure of Carmel, the absence of distraction, sharpened its edges intolerably. By the grace he gave me at the moment of conversion, he had, so to speak, 'killed' creatures for me. He knew well with what hungry passion I would fall on them only to find them cheats, but not before I had ruined them and myself. No ideas of God could touch me. I wanted him, the living God, wanted him to be bound to my inmost self, to be one with him—I knew not how—but there must be no 'separation', no 'space' between. Lovely thoughts, those acts of faith and love, remained 'outside' me, mysteriously deepening the sense of loss, absence. 'This is for others, not for me. Others can drink of this fountain but it is barred to me. He is the God of others, he loves them, they please him, are dear to him, but I am outcast, cut off from him. He cares nothing for me.'

Indeed, had I any real assurance that he existed? Life, and my dim experience of it, was just too deep, baffling and suffering to be enclosed in glib words and concepts. I am not including the beloved figure of the gospels in that last phrase. God forbid! I hung on his words. It was his God I believed in. He had lived a human life, gone through it all, gone through death and then told us to have confidence. It was true, all would be well. 'Fear not.' And so I lived by these assurances, tried to live as if I believed and loved, but icy, fearful hands forever clutched and tore at my heart. How can I describe it? Jesus, too, was outside me. In my catechism I had learned that he was in heaven and in the blessed sacrament—not everywhere, not 'in' me. Therefore, to imagine I was with him, as St Teresa advised, to think of myself beside him in the garden, on the mountainside at night in prayer, one of my favourite reflections, was just imagination and untrue and I could not feed on untruth. Because there was a strong tradition supporting this way of praying and it was advocated by those who knew, St Teresa and others, I practised it but it remained 'outside-prayer' and I longed for 'inside-prayer'. I had to wait many years before I found an answer to this problem and could give myself wholly up to Jesus 'in' me. Alas, I feel I am describing all this very inadequately.

I was like a starving person wandering through a beautiful countryside laden with fruit, and having to pass by devoured with hunger, not because I could not take the fruit, but because it could not satisfy my hunger, only increase it. This was experienced more acutely on great feastdays; I almost dreaded them. God was offering so much and I could do nothing about it. The feast and its treasure would pass away and I be guilty of neglect. I could not bestir my thought or feeling. Often we would have exposition and I would feel I must spend all the time possible in prayer, and yet it was not prayer, only blank inertia and depression. Vaguely, too, at times, something seemed just about to break through, only to evaporate, leaving a slight touch of remembrance, indefinable, ungraspable. I would be seized with a feeling of desperation. Yes, I shrank from love because I dimly realised the suffering of being loved and not able to repay love: of enduring love. I have stated crudely a most delicate, most subtle movement of my heart, of my being. I have distorted it. Perhaps it is best to leave it as it is for the moment. Maybe it will be clarified later.

It is impossible to understand my life unless it is seen all the time against the background of black depression. This was my atmosphere. It was only a matter of degrees. It was like a blight and I could not understand it. In those days we did not think in terms of temperament or psychology. I concluded that there must be something wrong with my spiritual life. I had had no training. There was no one to teach me how to pray. If only someone would come along who knew both the way to God and my own heart. This sense of failing and lacking the proper aids in the spiritual life—as I thought— raised the question in my mind of transferring to another Carmel. We were in touch with one of an old tradition and I automatically but foolishly concluded that I would find there what I did not find in my own monastery. Sr Agnes, considering what I had been through, and the present troubled state of the community, was prepared to investigate the possibility of a transfer, but when it came to the point the sound realism which lies beneath my romanticism told me such a plan was foolish.

The heart of this depression seems to have been fear, fear not of this or that precisely, but an ultimate fear, fear of my relation to God. Unless one has security in the Absolute; unless there is ground to being and ground to my own being then any assurances, any 'security', is mockery. To enjoy anything is mockery. A condemned man faced with a good meal! How acutely I felt all this. Life seemed to be poisoned. Yet, given the fact of God and his revelation, what I was thinking and feeling was sin, displeasing to him . . . Oh, there was no way out. No way except complete trust, dropping below this immense misery into the mercy of God. Gradually, in the fine point of my being, I was beginning to do this. I am sure it was what enabled me to go on, and not just to go on but to grow, to improve in spite of psychic confusion and conflict. Years later, groping for words, I was to say: 'There is a citadel within me that never yields'. This is correct. It is not I who hold the citadel, but the living God.

It was very difficult not to give way to moods. I yearned for sympathy but there was no one with whom I could discuss the state I was in. I was so afraid and ashamed that I would not reveal it. It never occurred to me to doubt that I had a vocation. I seemed to take it absolutely for granted that I must stay in Carmel, yet I was conscious that anyone, really aware of what was going on inside, might think I had none. I would show my moods at recreation not in a blatant way, for I cared too much for my reputation, but skilfully. It was the same in choir. There were all sorts of little ways in which one could draw attention to oneself. I might have deceived others but I did not deceive myself and this fault deepened my sense of sin and failure.

I could not say the office with attention. Or was it that I would not, that I did not take sufficient care, make the effort? This thought would worry me. St Teresa's warning that anyone who cannot say her prayers with attention must know she is not fulfilling her vocation disturbed me. I must make up my mind, I would try, but I never succeeded, not to this day. I remembered some words of St Francis de Sales to the effect that to get up after a fall, over and over again, was more pleasing to God than if we did not fall. I grasped this; that the trust which would go on, in spite of continual failure, must please God. I live by it still.

If only God would give me one touch of his love so that I could really feel that he loved me! I prayed for this but found myself adding: 'only if it pleases you'. I could not pray for favours in prayer. All I wanted was love. I wanted to love God and I would only want what would enable me to love him. I began to realise that it might be God's plan that I should always bear this desolation. Over and over again I would tell him I was ready to do so provided it would lead to greater love. Never did I think I had deserved any favour but I knew that God does not give according to deserts.

The year before my final profession, James married and brought his bride to see me on the evening of the wedding. I was deeply moved to see him so changed, to see their radiant happiness. I thought of them going off together, to the intimacy of their first night. No sooner had they left the parlour than I burst into a fit of weeping. My own lot seemed utterly bitter. Nothing, nothing, nothing, bleak, cheerless, lonely. And yet I found myself turning in the darkness to him, telling him I would go on to the end of my days feeling loveless if it pleased him. Truly there was a citadel within held by the living God.

Often the image would spring to my mind of myself in a little boat without oar or sail, on the vast expanse of ocean beneath a midnight sky. There was a sense of terror at the loneliness, at the dreadful depth below, at the utter helplessness of my state, but also the glorious security, unfelt though it was, of being held and controlled by the unseen God. I knew that I would rather be in that little boat with 'nothing' than enjoy all that the world could offer me. I was wrapped around, clasped in mystery. Looking back I see great significance in this image. My sea was vast, swelling, full, but it was calm. In spite of sensible sufferings there was, in my depths, a serenity—call it a citadel. The time was to come when I was to be engulfed by storms, storms which threatened the citadel itself, but in the earlier part of my life the depths were serene.

My reactions to a brief sojourn in hospital bear witness to the fundamental contentment. For the first two days I was pleased with the change and the fuss made of me. To the nurses, young women of my own age more or less, I was an object of great interest, but soon there were no barriers. I heard their fun and chatter and several told me of their male friends and hopes. I could enter into it all but at the same time could not but realise that, purely through the gift of God, I was in a different dimension where God was the overpowering reality. Not that this was 'experienced', far from it. I experienced only the solid reality of the world around me, and yet on reflection, induced by events such as this, I clearly perceived that in this respect my life was different. By the time the third day came I felt I could not wait another moment before returning to Carmel.

I made my solemn vows on September 8th, 1951, six months later than the expected date. Some members of the community were not satisfied as to my fitness. This could have been an objective judgement and as such wholly understandable but, rightly or wrongly, I suspected that it was not objective. The challenge was good for me. I pulled myself together and tried to get real control of myself, hiding my moods and cultivating a calm exterior. The very fact that I accepted this disappointment seemed to bring its own grace, for I was peaceful and happy.

The long retreat preceeding my profession was likewise happy. I took the retreat of Sr Elisabeth of the Trinity for my inspiration and found her helpful. I felt drawn also to our Lady at this time. I made my vows 'until death' with great resolution. Yes, I was happy. I remember being with the community on the morning of my profession and looking out onto our poor, ill-kept garden. I was here for ever. In one sense an appalling prospect but, contrary to all reason, I found myself content.

Shortly after my profession, M. Teresa left the community to return to her former monastery. At the time I judged her harshly but now I see things differently. She was a well-meaning person but was unable to cope with anything but a small situation. She had lost her balance and it was obvious she could not regain it in our community. Community opinion had veered away from her and turned fully to M. Agnes. She must have felt extremely lonely and hurt. We did not help her sufficiently but I doubt if whatever we had done would have been accepted. I am sure she was justified in leaving in order to start afresh and become herself again. She died about five years afterwards.

There were other departures in the next few years, but worse was Sr Patricia, who stayed on. I saw, reflected in her, what I might become. She was a classic example of the nun St Teresa describes so graphically in chapter 7 of *The Foundations* as suffering from 'melancholy'. The heart of the trouble is a craving for attention and to have one's own way. This sister, consciously and still worse, unconsciously, demanded attention. Endless the scenes, endless the physical illnesses that assailed her. Poor M. Agnes. As infirmarian I had much to do with this poor sister and was to learn a lot. I could enter into her and perhaps as no one else could as, basically I was prone to the same ills. She forced me to take a still firmer hold on myself and to shun any attempt to pose, play-act or seek attention.

The demonstrations of this sister were but a desperate cry for a solution to her problem. She was totally unfitted for the life which was a veritable imprisonment for her. A sensible priest was later to encourage her to leave, which she did, to become a normal member of society.

I cannot say that, apart from the new testament, any book helped me in a special way. Later on I was to study St Thérèse and find my sister-soul and guide. At this time I was groping alone. But I have a retentive mind and a power of assimilation. I would come across an idea, a maxim, an insight in my reading and, by instinct, would know it was for me. I have mentioned the influence of St Francis de Sales. There were other words of light which sank into me and became part of me. I might have forgotten they were there. Only later on, when conversing with and helping others, they would spring up naturally from my memory. Fifteen years later than this, an experienced priest, with whom I had much to do, remarked: 'You must have read very widely'. I thought for a moment and then replied: 'No, I have not read widely, I have read few books but have assimilated what I have read or heard'.

Looking back, I see that it was in God's providence that I should not find much help in spiritual writers but should stumble on alone. When upset or discouraged by what I heard or read on the spiritual life and way of prayer, I would turn for reassurance to the gospels. I collected our Lord's words on prayer. How simple they were. Why couldn't we leave it at that? Why must all these books be written? Deep in my heart, though I felt a compulsion towards them through anxiety, they repelled me. They made the way to God seem 'professional' and unreal. I can see that I could easily have fallen into the trap of seeking a spiritual life, seeking contemplation, seeking to be a woman of prayer. Our Lord saved me from this artificiality. I would indulge in it from time to time but sheer helplessness brought me back to truth. At this time I did not see clearly that this was truth. I was far too insecure. I despised myself too much to feel that anything I did, thought or practised was likely to be authentic. How great has been my need of someone to come along and affirm the deep insights which were growing within me.

7

LIVING LIGHT

Following the long-drawn-out ice-bound winter of 1952, which tried our patience to the limits, came the most glorious summer I have ever known, stretching from May, when the last streaks of snow melting in our garden revealed spring already there, until the end of October. It was harvest-time when M. Agnes took me on one of her house-hunting trips. She had conceived the daring idea of moving the Carmel into the country. Considering the total absence of funds, it was a courageous decision but wholly in line with her determined character, which could remain untouched by criticism or contrary opinion. This was my first glimpse of the countryside since my entry into the monastery seven years earlier. I was enchanted with the golden scenery, the corn cut and cocked, the stubble gleaming in the sunshine. There was an air of richness, contentment. The house in question, beautiful in itself, stood in gracious surroundings. Yet it was without regret that I returned to our poor little Carmel, shut in between houses. The thought of a Carmel in the country was lovely but I never found myself setting store by it. I realised that Carmel was independent of situation and it was Carmel that held me. What did I mean by 'Carmel'? It is too early to define this, for at this stage in my life I would have been incapable of defining it. The years that followed were an exploration of this concept and an attempt to establish it in its purity. I found in my heart that sense, I could call it experience, that I really had everything. All that lovely countryside, and other vast ranges of it that I would never see save in magazines or in imagination, was somehow mine. I had no sense of loss. The fact that I could not see or feel it did not matter. Dimly I was experiencing that having God one had all things. I was not in the least aware that I had God—all was dark and empty—yet this corollary dimly revealed to me that, hidden though he be, he was

87

truly there.

This particular house proved beyond our possibilities and, undaunted, M. Agnes looked for another. Towards the end of the year a much more modest dwelling was found and—I cannot say 'purchased' for we had no money—a contract was made and a small sum paid. It was hoped that the sale of the town house would bring sufficient to meet the cost. In actual fact it did not but somehow or other we managed to pay. M. Agnes with the stronger half of the group, among whom was myself, moved in early in March 1953. By this time our community consisted of ten choir nuns and two lay sisters. Our former companion of the novitiate, Stefana, was not accepted for final profession. A tiny group but, for that reason, a small house sufficed. I can still feel the sense of wonder when, early next morning, we knelt in the bare room which was to be our choir for the morning hour of prayer. I had only to turn my head to see the countryside stretching out before me. Oh, it was cold, but cold was so much easier to bear. And what a landscape it was!

Our monastery is situated on the foothills and known to command one of the finest views for miles around. To the west are the mountains—the everlasting mountains—reared against the sky, and over these the setting sun poured its splendours. To the south stretches the loveliest valley imaginable. From an eyrie cell I can watch spring dancing through the valley, the snows melting at her approach. No carefully laid-out gardens surround our house. Here nature runs riot. Masses of snowdrops and crocusses cover the ground in spring, then hundreds of daffodils and delicate narcissi. In spring and early summer the place is a mass of blossom. The lime trees surrounding the courtyard fill every room with fragrance. Amid so much loveliness the most enchanting thing of all is a wild, wooded ravine, a swift stream fresh from the mountains, singing in its depths. How can I describe it?

Bracken slopes and, oh joy, bluebells! I first caught sight of it of a sudden through the trees on the opposite bank—a sea of misty blue which could be nothing but bluebells, so beloved of my childhood. Every manner of flower graces this lovely place; forget-me-nots bluer than the heavens, meadowsweet, gorse, willow-herb, tangles of honey-suckle and fountains of wildrose. There are flowering trees too, wild damson and cherry which make you catch your breath as you come upon them in a bend of the path. Never shall I forget the thrill of our first discoveries but the charm has not faded.

My parents were delighted at the move. 'To think', my father mused, 'that you people had accepted to stay in that shut-up place all your lives and then God takes you out and gives you this'. He was voicing my own sentiments. I was prepared to stay in the town house but was deeply grateful that he had fulfilled a wish I had always cherished and seemed to renounce completely—to live in the country. He saw that my temperament needed this alleviation and certainly life was much happier. M. Teresa's departure, sad though it was, and a little later Sr Patricia's, removed some painful elements from our community life. There were still strains and tensions but no 'bad spirit' and this was a relief for us all.

Soon after our establishment at B-- we decided to keep a tiny herd of goats, the local, shaggy, mountainous breed which yet have a commendable milk yield, in order to supply ourselves with milk and butter. It was my charge. I found it intensely interesting. It was the first natural interest I enjoyed in Carmel. My occupations hitherto had been of a very humdrum character. This was different.

It put me in touch with nature in a more vital way. Everything had deeper significance. The first show of green grass after the long snows, the early buds on woodland shrubs, these were greeted with delight because my goats needed them. I glimpsed the marvellous harmony of nature and became in some way a child of nature. I delved into herbal lore and the medicinal properties of the common- est flower, weed or bush. I discovered the lavishness and loving care of God. What man and animal needed was there at their feet; the most valuable medicinal plant, the elder, was commonest, could not be got rid of but would obstinately spring up everywhere. In the autumn I would gather nuts and berries and fill the barns with hay, dried herbage and leafy branches ready for the dearth of winter. And the animals themselves—their warm, firm, vital flesh—sheer sense-life, whimsical creatures. As for the kids, well, there is a danger of wasting hours watching them play, leap, whirl, essay a fight. They are beautiful little creatures. The matings, then looking for the first signs of gestation, waiting for the birth, all this enthralled me. More than once I have spent the night among the goats, sleeping on a mound of straw. A moving experience. I could imagine myself in the woods and forests among the wild things of nature whose hidden laws, communications, feelings are known only to their creator. How little we know really of the animal world! I used to have deep thoughts watching my goats...Then too there was the satisfaction of supplying the community with plenty of milk and butter.

In the early years of B-- I did a lot of hard manual work. I made up my mind to it. I was the youngest in the community and, I thought, the strongest. M Agnes tended to protect me, claiming that I overdid things and was not equal to really hard work. One part of me liked this attention but the more honest part rejected it. There was no reason whatever why I could not put my back into work. I made up my mind to carry the burden and to shirk nothing. I think I did this. What is more, I accepted responsibility for the upkeep and wellbeing of the community. Gone were the days when automatically I felt there were others bearing the responsibility; others to fall back on, with me only a newcomer. I realised instinctively and correctly that a great weight of responsibility lay on my young shoulders.

In those days horizontal relationships were non-existent. If they took place they were illegitimate. It followed that we did not really know one another. We had only appearances to go by and the opinion of the prioress. If a prioress were to consider a certain sister lacking in humility etc, the rest of the community was likely to accept this as a fair judgment of one in a position to know. The upsetting of ordinary routine in the move and early days at B-- inevitably threw us together more. Recreations were often spent working in the garden and, as there were so few of us, the custom of always waiting until there were three before beginning to speak was abrogated. Thus two could lawfully speak together and now and then personal exchanges were made. Thus I came to understand sisters who were considered difficult and see there was nothing but goodness in their heart.

When M Agnes had completed six years of office, exhausted as she was with the labours involved in the move, she was replaced by M. Gertrude. This sister had filled the office of subprioress for

many years, first in her own community and then under M Teresa at
P--. She was an elderly person, completely dedicated, but timid and
scrupulous. She had an unbounded, completely non-critical trust in
whoever was prioress. To be appointed prioress meant that one was
automatically endowed with special wisdom and stood in the place of
Christ. She was utterly consistent in her own conduct and taught the
same to others. Hence when she herself became prioress, more than
any other, she expected absolute and unquestioning obedience. Her
timidity made her extremely narrow. She was incapable of looking to
right or left. She had an idea of the faithful religious and any
modification of this was quite unthinkable. In particular, any show
of independence or private judgement indicated that a sister was on
the downward path.

One of our confessors at this time was an exceptionally able man.
He enjoyed the confidence of almost the whole community and gave
sound, substantial help. I never set eyes on him and deliberately
refrained from doing so. A curtain always shut off a clear view of the
altar. Fr Conrad had a fine, strong, masterful voice. It was this that
impressed me.

Here was a man, and a man who knew what he was about, where
he was going and how to get others there. Was this the answer to my
secret prayer that God would send me someone to teach and guide
me? I began to seek his direction. He took a great interest in me and
this, in itself, was extremely gratifying. I tried to tell him about
myself, my struggles, my inability to pray. He gave me good advice
but I was unable to accept it. I had no conviction that he really
grasped 'me' and, indeed, I could not be wholly frank. I was too
afraid of myself, too ashamed to be utterly self-revealing even
though I tried to be. But I found great satisfaction in him. I began to
worry about this. I was no fool and could perceive clearly enough
that I liked having this man's attention. Was this right? Was it not a
dishonouring of my vow of chastity? I was very troubled. Besides
being subprioress I had been appointed assistant novice mistress
and at this time we had a postulant. My views on how to treat her
were clashing with M. Gertrude's and I spoke to Fr Conrad about it.
I remember the extraordinary sense of relief when he supported my
view and remarked that I must keep my own judgement, that the

91

prioress is not the only one guided by the Holy Ghost. It sounded blasphemous. I might not have accepted it from a less spiritual priest, but coming from this one I let it into my heart where it found ready assent. It was the beginning of my intellectual and emotional freedom.

A short while after this, I heard a sister in distress. She was crying in an utterly helpless, frustrated way and I went to the prioress to ask her to do something about it. As usual there was no response. I was angry and declared roundly that someone else might be right; she had not the monopoly of the Holy Ghost. I am relating this incident at length because it reveals an important element in enclosed religious life, an element rarely understood either inside or outside the monastery. Good M. Gertrude was utterly shocked, so much so that she was ill. Usually even-tempered, her face was now stiff and expressionless. There was no deliberate 'cold' treatment of me. She was just frozen. I could stand it no longer and broke the ice. She poured out her distress. That I should talk like that! Where was Carmelite obedience? I was going downhill rapidly ever since I gave my confidence to Fr Conrad. Priests cannot understand our way of life. Here was I once again up against the enormous, subtle pressure of the immediate superior. Fr Conrad and his objective common-sense seemed far away. Who was right? Meanwhile I agonised and this agony went on for weeks and weeks. Was I really going downhill? My superior said so. I had always accepted as from God what she had to say. I prayed for mercy, prayed to be forgiven. I was a bad religious, one of those unfaithful ones we read about. I was only too aware of the pride, ambition, smouldering resentment and ugly thoughts which lurked in my heart, and now outside witness had pronounced judgement. On the other hand, I saw the injustice of her words. Which view was right? Need I say that the balance was heavily weighted towards the first. I decided that God asked me to renounce Fr Conrad. If I continued to go on with him I would be at loggerheads with my superior.

I told her this decision. She assured me that she did not intend me to break with him wholly but only to be on my guard. But her whole attitude had made it impossible for me to accept him as director. She was relieved at my decision. I surrendered fully, reaffirming my acceptance of her as God's representative in my regard. Needless to say, I now think this decision the wrong one but at the time it was, I think, the only one possible and therefore right. At his next visit I simply told him I did not wish to speak. He made a tactful enquiry whether it was due to anything he had said. I replied that he could ask the prioress. He did so and she told him, unashamedly, of what had happened. She told me afterwards what she had said and what he had said to her, pointing out that there was a danger of the superior overstepping her authority. She was unmoved. Priests do not understand our way of life! The fathers of the order would understand but not secular priests or priests of active congregations. It was a long time before I could rid my heart of resentment whenever I recalled this incident. Fr Conrad continued to come. I used to see the others going to him and long to go myself. I think he guessed something of my anguish because he would delicately introduce something in his conference which could be taken as a word of encouragement.

I was becoming conscious of my powers, of my gift for leadership and, when a new postulant was expected, felt I should be made novice mistress. This I considered a temptation and admitted it humbly to the prioress, M Agnes once again. I took it for granted that would end my prospect of being appointed, for M Agnes often pointed out that I was in danger of intellectual pride. But with great largeness of spirit, she did in fact appoint me. I had three intelligent novices under my care.

It was with a chastened, cautious spirit that I undertook my work in the novitiate. I felt a profound mistrust of myself, aware as I was of my desire for authority. Dressing in the morning I would say over and over again from my heart: 'Averte oculos meos ne videant vanitatem: in via tua vivifica me'. Looking back I quail at what I taught—the customs in which I myself had been drilled and all the outward forms of the good religious. It was a system of imposing on a person, from without, a way of behaving, thinking, judging. We were saying: 'This is what a good religious does, thinks and feels. This is what you must become. You must conform to this if you want to be a good religious'. However, sheer experience in dealing intimately with people at a spiritual level began to show me the falsity of this system of education. My first years as novice mistress, whilst hard on my poor victims, were valuable for me. I was not free to break away from the accepted methods. I was not prioress and, in those days, the office of novice mistress was completely subordinated to that of prioress. She could not act independently. But in preparing my instructions I found myself against difficulties. My need to get to the bottom of things; to present clear, well-thought-out discourses revealed the shallowness of accepted notions. My mind was further stimulated to search for understanding. There was little to help me in the way of literature.

I was thirty one or two years of age when I faced a new crisis. There came into my hands a brochure of another Carmel. The photographs, the text—all spoke to my heart. This was Carmel. This was what my heart yearned for. Oh, why had God brought me to where there was nothing. No one to teach me, no one to whom I could look and say: 'You know the way. I see what Carmel has done for you. Help me'. I could see nothing that justified all that was said and written about Carmel. As usual, I turned to God in my distress. We were in retreat and so I had long periods of solitude. And then there surfaced clearly in my mind what I had always vaguely seen but never laid hold of. This *was* Carmel. Here there was indeed nothing—no security, no 'glory', nothing to give satisfaction. I had vowed poverty and I had it. I had declared myself ready to depend on God alone and he had taken me at my word. This was religious life in the raw, so to speak, and this was the essence of Carmel. Oh, if I had entered what I happily dreamed of as a perfect Carmel, with its fine tradition, its cloisters, I would have sought security in these externals, assumed the image of the Carmelite and escaped from God's working in me. There had been no mistake;he had not let me down; this was the set-up I needed, where I would be open to him. All this came with the thrust of certain truth. I surrendered my reservations and determined to give myself wholly to my 'poor' little community, to share its fortune for good or ill. This insight never failed me. I lost all desire for the 'ideal' condition, the 'ideal' Carmel.

Searching for the truth about Carmel, wanting to live this special way of life in an authentic way, I tried to appraise the situation in the light of what I understood. The major question in my mind was whether the stress on prayer was sufficient to warrant our withdrawal, as dedicated women, from the field of apostolic work. It seemed to me that there must be, in fact, a great difference between the life of a contemplative and an active sister. If the former found herself just as busy, just as occupied as a sister in an active congregation, how could her withdrawal from the apostolate be justified? The busy contemplative would be working merely to support herself and her family, and was a religious justified in doing merely this? I saw that, at B--, we were in danger of being over-active. My own work was demanding but I tried not to let it dominate me. Not only did I try never to be missing from the formal hours of prayer but tried to pray during my work, and as I spent a lot of time alone, in garden or woods, I tried to pray explicitly. As a community, under M. Agnes' guidance we were very faithful in limiting our work to working hours and not encroaching on prayer time. We took a risk in doing this and God rewarded it. Our income was higher than it had ever been, even though we were fewer hands. I am glad to have had experience of a very active outdoor life. I recall the aid it was to healthy balance, but at the same time I see that it was not wholly conducive to the contemplative life as understood in Carmel. Later I was to stand firm against keeping live-stock within the enclosure. Necessity has no law and I am not hereby saying I think the keeping of animals detrimental to the spirit of Carmel, but my own experience taught me that, if other ways of providing for the community can be found, this should be avoided.

Cut off from the world outside and items of news being rare, any tale of suffering and horror makes a strong impact. I would identify emotionally with the victims. As I have mentioned when speaking of my childhood, the sense of world distress was very great. In Carmel it became most acute. My thoughts were continually with the inmates of concentration camps, the people of Hungary, prisoners condemned to death and the like. Why should I be free from such trials, have all I needed, food, shelter, bed when so many others were plunged in such misery? I spoke to Fr Conrad about this and he gave me excellent advice which I have held on to since. He pointed out that identifying with them brought them no help and was damaging to myself. God was with each of them individually. They had graces which I had not. I was putting myself into their situation, but I was not them. There was falsity in this position. I must pray for them and live my vocation as fully as possible and in this way I would be helping. The fact remains that I do not think I could be so utterly happy as to forget that others are unhappy; the sorrow of others must always darken our lives and this, I think, is as it should be.

I also began to realise that we, in Carmel, share the inner sufferings of the world outside. I began to see that I was but one of many who suffered from depression, the inability to face life, fear, the sense of God's absence. When I set myself before God it was as the representative of a multitude, or rather, I held the multitude in my heart. This was not a forced thing, it came naturally to me and yet it was allied, as I have said, to a sense that I was not personally loved by God but was one of a vast crowd. Well, I did the best I could with this feeling and held the crowd in my heart before him. I comforted myself with the gospel incident of his mother being on the edge of the crowd whilst others pressed him close. Others could be near him; she was left on the fringes. As the years went by this involvement with others, to the point of self-loss before God, was to grow in intensity. It seemed the only way I had of being in touch with God. I could never ask anything for myself alone. I realised that there was something unbalanced in this attitude but there was nothing I could do about it. It was making a virtue of necessity.

As I have matured in the spiritual life, so I have come to understand more and more the meaning of the contemplative apostolate. Many, many times I have felt that my life was utterly useless; only the testimony of the church, especially in its solemn affirmation at the Vatican Council, reassured me, but now I grasp in a more than notional way that, when one is open to God one is opening the world to God; when one is totally surrendered, everyone else is more surrendered too. If I let God take hold of me more and more; possess me, as fire possesses the burning log, then I give off light and heat to the whole world even though the influence be completely hidden.

Prayer always presented enormous problems. I was utterly confused about how to pray. As I have said earlier, I yearned for inward prayer, to find my God in uttermost intimacy, and was faced with nothing. If I tried to be quiet in prayer I was conscious only of myself. Introspection was a tyranny and I felt this was my fault. At the same time I vaguely knew that, if I could find myself, I would find my God. I did not know how to 'enter within myself'. I seemed shut out from myself. It was this drawing inwards which made meditation on the sacred humanity of our Lord a difficulty. I wanted to pray to God-within-myself, whatever that might mean, but Jesus seemed in the way. I wanted to go out to the infinite, beyond thought, to know myself engulfed by the infinite God, and Jesus seemed in the way. I was worried about this. Jesus' own words, 'No one comes to the Father but by me' were real to me. I knew that it was only because of him that I could say 'Our Father'; that he said it with me. It was only in the act of prayer itself that I was passing him by . There was support for this 'way' in such works as the *Cloud of Unknowing* and much Carmelite literature on prayer. The prayer of loving attention would presume this absence of consciousness of the sacred humanity. But St Teresa would have none of it. She is explicit on the subject. Not only did her words warn me but my own heart also. I was uneasy. I spoke to our chaplain. He confessed himself unable to answer as there was tradition on both sides. For some years I wavered between the two, never confident enough to give myself to the deeper sort of prayer described in the *Cloud* yet, when dwelling on our Lord's life, longing for it. The dilemma was solved for me. When I was engulfed in bitter trials later on, I found I just could not go 'direct' to God—there was no meaning in such an approach. Jesus became my all. Without any 'experience' I yet understand that we can go to God directly only in Jesus. We cannot sidestep.

In the effort to live a truly prayerful life, I tried to control my nervous, over-eager temperament. When I found myself getting worked up and agitated I would pause, take a hold on myself and deliberately act calmly. The more I had to do the more I refused to 'let go' of myself. I learned too to keep things in perspective, not to fret because the hay was lost, the sowing late, the milk yield down, a goat sick or dead. Ultimately all that mattered was that we should

love God, the rest was peripheral. There was a time when it seemed
we could not carry on, that we were fighting a losing battle and the
words of the 'Canticle of Habakkuk' which we recited occasionally in
the office, struck me as strikingly relevant and I made them my own.
To use a modern rendering:

For though the fig tree blossom not nor fruit be on the vines,
Though the yield of the olive fail and the fields produce no
harvest,
Though the flocks disappear from the fold and there be no herd in
the stalls,
Yet will I rejoice in the Lord and exult in my saving God.

God was to respond fully to our trust.

Thrown full tilt into nature, delighting in sight and sound, I
pondered on the question of how a wholehearted christian, and
especially a Carmelite, should regard created things. I was reading
the old testament and very much struck by the unashamed delight in
things of sense, food, drink, sex. These were seen as God's gifts and
enjoyed. This attitude was far removed from the one we had imbibed.
I felt a strong pull to this world. I belonged to it. I wanted it, wanted
to delight in it; to experience the 'good' life such as was pictured as
an ideal in the old testament. But was it so upheld in the new? Here
there was a sense of greater detachment, an urgency. We do not
really belong here, do not delay, pass on, touch everything lightly.
What is more, the shadow of the cross lies over created reality. I
found it very difficult to establish a proper view. I looked at our
Lord's infancy and childhood and even there one found the cross.
Close to the blissful night of Christmas was the feast of the
Innocents, recalling the bloody massacre and the mothers' anguish.
And yet our Lord clearly loved this world, found delight in it. He
attended village feasts and rich men's banquets. He watched the
children playing in the market-place. He too must have played as a
child. He took it for granted that the majority of the men and women
he was speaking to would go on living ordinary lives, eating,
drinking, marrying, sowing their fields, reaping their harvests and,
in their own measure, enjoying life. But what of us Carmelites? Our
whole ethos seemed a denial of creatures. Carmel is the desert and
there is a minimum of created comfort in the desert. Was our

attitude wholly compatible with the gospels? I did not know and went on thinking. I wanted to say a wholehearted 'yes' to the created world and to delight in the created world. It was not of first importance that I should enjoy creatures, enjoy the 'good life'. Lying behind this question is a true or false image of God. There is surely something terrible, outrageous, in the thought of a God who fashioned our nature, gave us bodies and senses, filled the world with so many beautiful, attractive things and then bade us renounce them and try to live as though we had no bodies. Has God really made a mistake? Has he regretted giving us bodies? Much of spiritual teaching, almost every book of asceticism one picked up gave this impression. The further one could withdraw from matter, and this includes our own bodies, indeed especially our own bodies, the better. This was the way to become spiritual and approach God. What an idol, what a distortion! I revolted against it.

Our chaplain at this time used to give us conferences. He was a highly intelligent man and a searching spirit. Clearly he had many problems in his emotional and spiritual life and was struggling to find an answer to them and to those of other people, for he had a heart of compassion. He was one of those who heralded the Council, raising the questions and essaying answers which were to become part of the message of Vatican II. Cautiously he would throw out some of his ideas. They found fertile soil in me. I remember a conference on our Lady in which he questioned, delicately and humbly, whether she knew that her child was God. Some of the community were shocked. I was not and pondered on it and our Lord's human experience. All this was relevant to my problem.

During this period, as I have said earlier, there was smooth continuity, not violent change. The difficulties continued but so did God's grace. I think it was at the Christmas of 1950, or thereabouts, that my parents gave me a copy of the letters of St Thérèse in an English translation. This volume threw new light on Thérèse. She was more real, more human, more like ourselves. I was struck by her marvellous heroic charity but also by the tenderness of her personal relationships. She was not afraid of expressing her love. At this time, too, I had come across an account of the life of her young novice. It was a rough translation into English of a 'death notice' sent to all the Carmels from Lisieux. I was always painfully conscious of the gulf existing between Thérèse and myself but I could recognise myself in the emotionally immature novice with whom she had to deal. I was comforted to see how Thérèse encouraged her, how tenderly and understandingly she trained her. This gave me new heart. Our great Teresa might have disowned me (or so I thought at the time) but little Thérèse would have understood me and helped me to grow. But these were side-lines compared with the great insight I gained from two of the letters in particular. They answered my deepest need. I recognised myself and my deepest convictions in them.

What God wants from us above all is trust, that trust which is our profoundest homage to him. He wants us to believe utterly in his will to load us with blessings. He wants us to let him love us. Most spiritual people learn to see his loving providence in the events of their lives, hidden though it may be, but it is a different matter when it comes to their interior states. They find it extremely difficult to believe that he is there, offering his love to them in their present, seemingly unsatisfactory prayer. This absence of all feeling, all high stirrings, this absence of the sublime leads them to think, even if secretly, that something has gone wrong, that they are spiritual failures. Rarely is their distress due to love of God, rather it is because it makes them feel so poor and good-for-nothing. They flee from this state and, in so doing, escape from God. Perhaps they throw themselves into self-sacrificing activity for others, sparing themselves in nothing. Now they are doing something for God! Or maybe a rigid form of conduct, avoiding all possible risk of failing in obligation, may be the channel of escape. It may be possible to work up some sort of fantasy prayer which deceives themselves if not others. What God is asking is that they should accept to be loved utterly not because they are good but because he is good. They want to earn his love. They hate to feel they do nothing for him and must receive love as a free gift. The purest love of God accepts one's being just as a receptacle—Thérèse would say a 'victim'—to receive this outpouring of God's love, and the more poor and wretched we are the more we are fitted for that. 'Let us keep far away from all that glitters'. How few people are really convinced that the 'experiences'

100

described in treatises on prayer are in no way essential for perfect prayer. Most well-instructed people will pay lip service to this, and encourage others in their darkness and aridity, but in their heart of hearts they are not really convinced, as can be seen by their great interest and curiosity about 'experiences', their tendency to speak with bated breath of any instance they know of, the tendency to think holy anyone whom they think enjoys these favours. True prayer is a giving of self to God, an opening of the self to God, not a seeking to feel God and his action.

I think that, in these days, we must have the courage, which can only flow from conviction that prayer has nothing to do with what is 'experienced', to shake ourselves free from the ideas almost uniformly presented by mystical writers of former days. Is there one who does not speak as if some sort of 'experience' must crown a spiritual life, otherwise something has gone wrong? We need to turn back to the gospels and our Lord's simple statements on prayer. We need to look around at people whom we know are leading dedicated lives, devoted to prayer. The common experience will be of 'absence', darkness, nothing. How foolish to conclude that this denotes something wrong, that we moderns have lost something, that God seems less concerned about us than about earlier generations. It seems to me we can trust that God, faithful to those he loves, longing only to give himself, is positively choosing to give himself in this dark way, this poor way.

It is easier for some natures to trust God than for others. They have a basic security and, in spite of difficulties, life is experienced as good. But for others of a less robust and solid structure it is much more difficult. If a pewter mug and an egg shell china cup were conscious, their experiences would be very different. The latter would live with a sense of peril. So the fragile nature has no natural foundation for trust and when it truly trusts in God its trust is pure. The more solid nature cannot know how authentic is its trust in God until its inner security is taken away and it is reduced to a similar state of deprivation and fragility. It may well be God's plan to do something of this kind, and alas that the one so blessed should seek to escape from this suffering.

Sometimes God will bring a person to poverty precisely through 'favours'. He knows what is best for each of us. The mistake would be to seek them as something valuable. They are valuable only if God wills them for us. Some plants need a lot of sun and rain to bring them to their full beauty, whilst others rot if they are given more than a minimum. For my part, I know I must welcome every experience of weakness, every opportunity I get for learning how helpless I am. My life has been sorrowful but it has been life. I have lived. Life has not passed me by.

8

CHRIST LIVES IN ME

My thirty third year began a new era in my life. On the one hand it was rich, overflowing, on the other pervaded with bitter suffering. It would not be inaccurate to sum it up as my discovery of womanhood, its pain and its glory. God brought me face to face with my sexuality. I do not use this word in a purely physical sense but as denoting that particular, all-pervasive moulding of human nature as male or female. God led me in this way to an ever greater grasp of the truth of my being, to accept my sexuality and open it to him.

In 1962 I was chosen by the community as their prioress. My sentiments on this day were humble. I could not deny that I wanted to be prioress and this, in itself (according to St Teresa) seemed a lack of virtue. Such a one was the last person to be governing others. I had been told often enough that I was prone to intellectual pride. All the same, I turned to God with great confidence and asked him, just because it was so incongruous, to look after things and help me, in spite of my pride and ambition, to be a good prioress. I prayed this with all my heart and in such a way that I knew my prayer was answered. I held on to this assurance through the difficulties which lay ahead, not only difficulties from without but interior difficulties which made me feel so often that, in spite of appearances, I was an utter failure and the whole situation a mockery. No glory attached to being prioress of the poorest, smallest, most insignificant monastery in the country if not the world.

The first thing I wanted to do was to make the sisters happy. I wanted to create such an atmosphere of mutual trust between the prioress and the sisters and among the sisters themselves—I saw how much the latter depended on the former—that each one would have the unconscious security of being valued, trusted and loved. For the average person, and that is what most of us are, this is the atmosphere in which a true, deep prayer life can flourish. I have been prioress for some years and I have learnt how the two go together. It is only the gifted person who can thrive in spite of an unhappy environment. Above all, the eremitical spirit, essential to Carmel, needs this warm, trusting atmosphere. If people are vaguely conscious they are objects of suspicion, if they are lonely in a way religious should never be, then solitude becomes a purgatory. A contented nun is happy in solitude.

Only in an atmosphere of acceptance can a person reveal herself as she is, and thus grow in understanding of herself and be open to development. In fact, all virtues flourish where there is trust. The more people are trusted the more responsible and honourable they become, at least that is what my experience has proved.

I know that as far as one can humanly judge such things, I have been a successful superior but the Lord has kept me weighed down interiorly under such a burden of well-nigh unbearable affliction and humiliation that my outward success has scarcely touched me, beyond causing feelings of satisfaction and vanity which but humbled me the more.

Speaking of this success suggests a digression which is nevertheless important and useful. As prioress I have come into contact with other communities of Carmel and understood something which is rarely understood. Often enough, the one chosen for the office of prioress is a woman of personal charm and magnetism. It seems that many, if not most communities, at some point of their history, have been governed by such a one. She is a natural leader and enjoys a natural ascendancy. She is the sort that the majority of the community will have no difficulty in accepting and in obeying. This personal magnetism is normally joined with some spirituality and this enhances it. Now we have a situation of great peril for the one in question and proportionately for her community. The natural 'radiance' is confused with holiness. 'There is something special about our mother, our Lord shines through her'. The truly holy, God-possessed person, lacking this natural brilliance, veiled perhaps by natural defects, often passes by unnoticed. Unless such a superior knows herself, unless she sees that what is impressing others within and without the community, is merely a natural thing and, in itself, nothing to do with holiness, she will be deluded. I fear more than one has fallen victim to this blindness. She has begun, secretly, to think of herself as special, as under the special inspiration of the Holy Spirit and therefore her utterances, her judgments, her commands have an elements of infallibility about them. She will appear to be most concerned with humility, deceiving herself and others that she is truly humble, but an honest appraisal of her conduct will reveal gross injustice and lack of charity, or at least, a blindness which brings into question any close union with God. Such a one is playing a role, ready always with the right, spiritual answer. Oh, how utterly destructive is flattery, how dangerous is authority! May God never let me be deceived into thinking I am other than I am.

Probably I have made it sufficiently clear already that, from my girlhood, I was aware and pleased with my femininity. Brought up in a family of girls, I had no sense of inferiority whatever. My father was the eldest of his family and hence we came on the scene before our cousins. We were made much of by grandfather and our admiring uncles and aunts. On my mother's side we were the only children. In the neighbourhood, in the parish we were admired. It was only in Carmel, in relation to the ecclesiastical world with its discrimination—contempt almost—for women, that I met this problem head-on. However, it was really innocuous. It angered me but had not the slightest effect in lessening my sense of woman's perfect equality with man. In many ways she seemed to me superior. I do not think I ever thought in terms of rivalry until I met this discrimination. Man and woman were taken for granted. In my own home I saw Mother and Father playing distinct but equal roles. In some areas—to do with us children, our education and so on—Daddy relied completely on Mother but she would take no decision without asking him and this dependence came naturally. It was not lip-service or mere duty. Father was definitely head of the household. Mother was the heart and ruled it by her heart. Daddy would talk over his business with her each day after dinner. She would listen patiently, putting in a word here and there. Then she would tell him of anything to do with us. She had been to see the headmistress, the doctor, and so on.

When I entered Carmel it struck me that some of the sisters had become mannish and I disliked this. These sisters did the heavier work. A huge sack apron over an enormous habit, heavy boots or clogs, the tendency was to stride around or develop a rolling gait. Instinctively, without much thought, I watched this. I was careful of my carriage and way of walking. I did not want to get 'tough'. At B--, shovelling coal, cleaning out goat and hen-houses, ploughing, carrying loads of hay on my back, I took care of myself. I strongly disliked having to have my hair cut very short and wept when it was done the first time after clothing. I felt ashamed. Later on, when I thought I was not disobeying by doing so, I let it grow a little.

I remember one evening at B-- when I was trying on a costume for St Joseph, I looked at myself in the large window. Our constitutions forbid us to use mirrors and it was considered an infidelity to use a pane of glass instead. I had never seen myself since I entered. I thought it would not be wrong to try out my beard and head scarf. Windows with the night outside are flattering and I was interested and pleased at the reflection given back. I took off my beard and had a good look. Somehow it seemed perfectly harmless. It was like looking at a third person. The word which came immediately to mind was 'elfish'. Years ago, I bought a picture for my mother. It was only the lid of a chocolate box and I bought it for sixpence. I liked it. It was the wistful, elfish face of a little girl selling violets. My mother liked it. She said:'It is so like you'. And that was the face looking back at me from the pane of glass.

It was not until I became prioress and was brought into contact with outside that I became overwhelmingly and painfully conscious of my potentialities and powers and...their seeming waste.

I came into contact with our then chaplain, Fr Karl, a man much older than myself. He revealed his immense compassion for us. A keen, original thinker, a rebel, ahead of his times, critical of authority and of the way the church authorities were, as he thought, distorting the image of God, he suffered from unresolved emotional conflicts. I loved his mind but could never trust his practical judgment nor accept him as a director on the spiritual level. But what a friend he was! Gently, humbly, without interference, he dropped hints as to what he thought in our set-up was archaic and ridiculous. This outside, objective opinion was a great help to me. I began to see things in the same light. They ceased to be sacrosanct. In fact, what he said usually coincided with my own view, which I dare not hold because of the weight of tradition and, to some extent, current authority. Furthermore, he stimulated my mind, encouraged me to think. He would send in any interesting review he received and invite my opinion. We used to meet about once a month to discuss theology and religious life. I can never do justice to what I owe him. He taught me to think carefully and clearly and not to make statements which I could not prove. With him I could show an open front. He was quite unshockable and he came to realise that I was also. Under his influence I unconsciously threw aside the image of the proper nun and prioress and let myself be my spontaneous self. 'Don't pretend', said he, 'that the office of prioress is a "heavy burden God has laid upon my shoulders"; you enjoy being prioress. Of course you do. You are cut out for it. If you are made for a job you are bound to want it. Go and bury your *Ah, ah, ah, ah, Domine,* in a big hole in the ground. You are a jolly good prioress'.

Can you imagine how pleasing this contact was after so many years of extreme seclusion and repression? There was no one in the community with whom I could really communicate. All of them were leaning on me to a greater or lesser extent. I was bearing a heavy burden and was utterly lonely. God gave me Fr Karl as a friend and outlet. His admiration of me was unfeigned and, knowing how critical he was, how hard to please when it came to a religious person, I was pleased and encouraged. I needed this external affirmation, so great was my insecurity in spite of the brave face I put on and the seemingly confident way I was tackling things. What is more, I vaguely knew he loved me and later on he was, in his shy, inhibited way, to tell me so. Our friendship lasted until his death. I was a person to whom he could pour out all his misery.

Yes soon, very soon, the roles were reversed. I never told him of my inner desolation. I realised I could not. He was deceived on that score and took me for what I seemed to be. The more he revealed his own uncertainties and distress, the less could I dream of seeking support in him. I have to admit that, in fact, he became a crushing burden which would, I think, have been unbearable, considering my own inner anguish, had not God sent someone to support me. Nevertheless, I never think of Fr Karl but with gratitude. He gave me his all and I think I proved a true and faithful friend. He wept at our last interview.

For a very brief period, Fr Bernard filled the role of chaplain, He was a religious man of some reputation as a director and from my small experience of him I realised he was extremely mortified and austere. He rather frightened me. At the same time I felt an inward compulsion to speak with him and that if I did not do so I would be refusing grace. My conviction that I needed a man's direction had never left me, and vaguely I was confident that God would supply my need. On the other hand, I feared possible involvement. It seemed to me inevitable that, if ever I trusted a man sufficiently to reveal myself to him, I would be emotionally involved. This did not seem likely in Fr Bernard's case as he was some twenty years older than me.

I was oppressed by my inner trials. I dreaded to reveal myself. Any director of insight would know me for the fraud I was. But then, was it not better to have my fears confirmed? God would still be there, and may be this priest would help me to find the right path. All this dreadful self-doubt and insecurity over-lay but never destroyed the basic surrender I have spoken of. Almost to this day, when I gave an account of myself to such a person, I would tell him only the misery, the seeming lack of faith, the absence of any real spiritual life, the incessant distractions. Secretly I would hope that the director would discern for himself what lay beneath (the basic attitude, I mean, or rather what I understand to be God's hold on my inmost being) and this would be a consoling affirmation for which I yearned. To speak of it myself would be presumption. It would give a wrong impression; would seem to cancel out the desolation and utter 'absence'.

At last I plucked up courage to speak. His response was indescribably gentle, sensitive and delicate. I tried to tell him just what things felt like. 'But', said he, 'it is so obvious God is with you, that the Holy Spirit guides you . . . you show amazing flexibility for a young superior . . . you are prudent and wise'. I could hardly believe my ears.

For the two months he remained with us I made use of him. He encouraged me with delicacy, heaping up compliments in an effort to counteract the appalling insecurity which he recognised. He used to reproach me for the 'bad habit of self-depreciation'. All this was delectable food for a starving woman and I ate it ravenously. Too ravenously. I could not have enough of it, alas.

When Fr Bernard left us I felt utter desolation. I had lost him although he assured me that I had not. We agreed that I should write to him several times a year, about every two months in fact. His letters became the only thing I cared about. For once I could open my heart. Here was immense, delicate appreciation of the real me. No one else knew me, knew the desperate, frightened, fragile self. Fr Bernard held me in his hands as one holds a fragile vessel—and with the same detachment. I was to complain that he held me with the tips of his fingers and that, at every moment, I expected him to let me drop. He assured me that he would never do that.

I was left with my womanhood all uncovered, raw, aching. All that happened in these few years, crammed as they were with experience, had brought to the surface the yearnings of my nature. As I have said earlier, I felt but a half-thing, without meaning, torn, rent and bleeding. It was experienced physically as a sense of tearing around my chest, as though I were being hollowed out. And there seemed no answer, no hope of alleviation. I turned to God as I always did but no conscious help was given, only the strength to go on, to hide my torment from others, to help them, to listen to their own griefs whilst my own being was shrieking with loneliness and pain. It was a help to me, I am sure, to have others to care for. It forced me to control myself. Each Sunday, in all weathers, I would make the stations of the Cross in the garden. Here I could be alone, here I could give vent to my feelings, weep and cry to God. I would take an hour or more, drawing from our Lord the strength to go on. It seemed meaningless and cruel. This particular suffering was to remain for many years and underlay the other troubles which were heaped upon me. It was, I think, the source of the others and gave the others all their sting and sense of hopelessness.

What precisely was the nature of this severe suffering? I can see several causes. To take the more superficial ones: in the first place I was being psychically drained. At the time I knew nothing of this sort of thing. Later on, a psychiatrist pointed out to me that a lot of my depression derived from this fact. Inevitably I was being drawn on psychically—it belonged to my makeup and was what gave me my influence and power over others—but it left me exhausted with no energy to enjoy anything, no energy for any other experience. I think there is a lot of truth in this. Then, too, there was the loneliness of my position. Thirdly there was a suffering sexuality, as I have described. Yet I am sure that none of these, nor all of them together, explain it. The root of it was the sheer fragility of my being. Here was existential fear, the fear of existence itself. Here was threatened, meaningless existence. Later on I was to read something of Kierkegaard and others and recognise my own state in theirs. Fr Bernard was to exclaim: 'How well you write. Far better than the existentialists themselves!' All through the years that followed, though I sought help, hoped for help in this or that, in this person or that, deep in my heart I knew there was no remedy. My suffering lay at the very roots of existence which no mortal hand could reach. And God was utterly absent.

It seemed to me that the only possible remedy would be a great human love. This would enfold my frail being, affirm it, give it meaning, give it a name, give it eternity. This poor being of mine would be given to another and become itself in that other. An ideal, and purely an ideal! God, in his love, saw that, in fact, this would not happen and so preserved me and someone else from tragedy. However, this realisation of the power of love, its creative and fulfilling role, led me to seek what drops I could. I would pour out the desolation of my heart to Fr Bernard. He would write back speedily in his skilful, delicate way. His advice was always excellent and I learned much of the art of direction from him, but my chief concern was to detect a note of affection. It was usually there but, of course, totally inadequate, as I knew it must be. There was no question of my thinking of Fr Bernard as my other half. But he was a man, a man of great delicacy who had troubled to concern himself with my poor self. This was enough to awaken the hunger. This relationship continues, but has changed its character.

Looking back over these outpourings of desolation, I question their legitimacy. With my present light I judge them extremely selfish and to be avoided. In the first place, they do not alleviate the suffering. I had borne a great deal hitherto without a confidant and had come to no harm. Once I had a confidant, restraint became almost impossible. I craved for an adequate response, for some one to enter into the depths of my woe—in other words, to suffer it with me! As regards Fr Bernard, I thought only of myself. It did not occur to me that my letters might be a burden to him, as I am now sure they were. He was a man as sensitive as myself, subject to depression. It was precisely this make-up which made him so responsive. Knowing how Fr Karl had weighed me down, knowing how I have been weighed down by the burdens of others, I am resolved never to burden another with my own sufferings. Later on, I was to burden someone else, some one of a different make-up who, I felt, could bear the burden. But there can be no relief if the recipient is unresponsive and there can be no response if there is no affection, hence there must be wounding. I deeply regret now the selfishness which indulged in this outlet with little or no regard for what I was doing to the person who loved me. At the time it seemed justified. My burden was unbearable. That may well be but we have to be prepared to die for one another, to suffer anything rather than hurt another through selfishness.

When I recall the friends God has sent me I am filled with wonder and gratitude. He has chosen a hard, dark path for me but he has provided me with singularly fine friends. It was about this time that Dr F. came into my life. To him I spoke of my depression and the interior deadness into which I had sunk. It seemed as if my positive emotions had died. Nothing moved me, not even the beauty around me. I knew, objectively, that it was beautiful but it was far away from me. It was empty, cruel, mocking. What did it mean, all this beauty, when I was cut off from its source? I felt a dried-up, barren woman. Dr F. pointed out that my emotions, far from being atrophied were, in fact, intense. He could give me drugs which would ease the depression but would, at the same time, rob me of other, rich experiences. He tried to show me that I was experiencing life in a rich, intense way and that I was a full woman. 'Une femme inspiratrice' he used to say, 'and what a difficult role that is! You

111

inspire others but remain dried-up yourself'. All this was a comfort in one way but, in another, I was but tormented the more. I had a nagging sense of waste—all that potential wasted. The potential of my very body wasted. I found some relief in offering myself specifically as a woman, my body, sexual powers and emotions as well as my spirit, to the action of the Holy Ghost so that he would invade me as he did our Lady and make me fruitful. I am sure he heard this suffering prayer. This, I realise, is precisely what consecrated virginity is: the surrender of our sexual power and all that goes with it—and how very much goes with it—to God.

In one of my first interviews with Fr Bernard, I was saying something to the effect that I had been given, for one brief moment, a glimpse of the mountain top, veiled indeed, but a glimpse nevertheless—referring to the dark, powerful illumination of my seventeenth year. 'And you are still climbing the mountain? he queried. To which I made the surprising reply, 'In a way I have got there'. He was a little taken aback, I think, but then grasped what I was trying to say. Under the circumstances there was no subconscious desire to impress. I was far too aware of Fr Bernard's perception for that, and besides, I was seeking to know the truth. What I said sprang from my heart without reflection. I was to make a similar statement later and again recently. Each time I meant the same thing but with, I hope, deeper reality. What did I mean? I was referring to that profound surrender in trust; the surrender of poverty to God. I realised then, as I realise even more now, that this gave me to God and God to me. This was the essence of union, of sanctity. Not for a moment did I think I was perfect. Perfection has nothing to do with it. Given this profound hand-over, nothing can keep one from God. I expect to be imperfect to the end of my life and yet I am certain that God will accomplish in me all that he wills. It is the certainty that nothing can separate us from the love of Christ . . . that Power finds its full scope in weakness . . . that we are created and predestined by a God of love who seeks only to give himself to us. This was the rock on which my life was based. Usually it was submerged by the furious waves and I could not perceive it. I was conscious only of the darkness and the storm but, given the impulse, I could test its presence.

In later years I was to notice that it was in times of most acute doubt—when some person whom I trusted cast doubt on my state, and I was thrown into an anguish of self-doubt—it was then that I perceived this sure rock and knew, without knowing, that I was safe; that my spirituality was sure; that, in fact, I was closely united to God even though all my conscious experience gave the lie to it. I would perceive it too when others would speak of their fear of God's judgment. I have never known this fear. I have feared annihilation; feared, dreaded the utter otherness of God, but his condemnation never. My God is the God revealed in Jesus. It is impossible to conceive of him condemning me, not because I am good but because he is good, and I have cast myself on to the bosom of his goodness and have consented to remain always weak and poor so as to receive his love more freely. I have longed for death as the only way out, merely as an end to darkness, suffering, untold mystery and yet, deep down I have known that, for me, death would mean revelation, death would mean love...Oh, so hidden away were these convictions! They afforded me no comfort on the conscious level.

It must be understood that what I write about these sufferings is flowing over into the years that lay ahead. I think it is better to speak of them in one sweep. It is vital to the history of my life and God's work in me.

The works of St John of the Cross gave me strange comfort. Even to hold a volume in my hands imparted a sort of healing. I ventured into the *Spiritual Canticle* and especially the *Living Flame*. Never did I think that what he was speaking about corresponded to my own state. The discrepancies were far too great for that, but I found passages which could be adapted to fit my state. I have come to realise since that experiences in the spiritual life happen at various stages of growth in differing degrees.

I sought for light in the gospels. There I found words of life. I put all my faith in Jesus, in what he said about God. Without being able to satisfy my intellect, which always yearned for clear expositions, I dimly realised that he had sunk into the abyss, had shared the anguish of death. He had gone through it and then cried out: 'It is all right. It is God, it is heaven'. Only he had the right to say to us frail creatures 'fear not', because only he could guarantee our existence, our relation to the infinite. And this word, 'fear not', was strewn through the pages of the gospel. Truly our God knows the heart of man and knows that fear is his natural atmosphere. He has revealed to me the dreadfulness of human existence, the cliff-hanging aspect. In this way he has purified my faith and trust.

Fr Karl told me I was destined to pioneer and must accept this vocation. If I shirked it and was content to follow others, I would be failing God. Fr Bernard in his own way corroborated this. I tried to put my ideas in writing for community conferences. I remember that I often used the image of the sea and the story of Peter walking on the water at our Lord's call. That was an image of my life. The depth below—nothing but faith in Jesus and he, seemingly, at a distance. Also, I likened human experience, the experience of ourselves, to the last ripples which lap the beach, ripples of the mighty ocean of our being lost in God. Again I would use the desert imagery, drawing on the biblical stories of God's drawing his own to the desert and caring for them there. It is strange how those two images haunted me. My natural taste lies in the beauty of the familiar, homely countryside. There was a conflict here. Naturally I was longing for this world. I belonged to it, its dear familiar being, and yet my spirit passed beyond it and moved into the vast, terrible unknown. And yet, and yet, Jesus belongs to earth. His resurrection has sanctified this world of sight and sound and lovely touch. At this time I was unable to integrate the two attractions. In some way we never shall in this life. Tensions such as these are part of our human greatness.

Recently I had a dream. I, along with many other people of all sorts, was at the top of some building wanting to get down. Everyone was making for and using a moving, steel escalator, fragile looking but of proven safety. People were boarding it as a matter of course without any sense of fear, sitting and reading their newspapers. I was frightened of it. One could see the depth below, and even to board it we had to take a step, a tiny one to be sure, over the gulf. This I could not do but knew I was not asked to do it. Gaily, without any sense of shame, I made my way to the solid, closed-in staircase near by and, alone, ran down it. I think this dream is significant. What we cannot do God is not asking. He asks what we can do. I could not—and cannot—follow what seems the classical spiritual journey. God does not ask it of me. He has provided another way for me. It may appear a poor sort of way, even a cowardly one, but it is my way and his choice for me. More than that, I know that, ultimately, in its essence, it is the only way. Sooner or later everyone must be brought by him to this deep poverty, and everything depends on acceptance of it. Personalites, temperaments differ and God leads all according to their own character. Roads may appear different but ultimately they converge. Sooner or later we must take the narrow path and leave behind all our spiritual riches. We have to go to God with empty hands. We have to let him be wholly and totally God. How hard this is. We want to feel good, want to feel we have something to offer him of our own. We want to be spiritually beautiful, to have an interesting, beautiful spiritual life. In his mercy he deprived me of all from the beginning. He has kept me in a state of poverty and helplessness. Now he has given me the grace to want this, to choose it.

St Thérèse was to say that the suffering face of Jesus was the heart of her spirituality. A fact rarely alluded to. I can say the same. I have come to realise that the mystery of my own life lies here. From the first he has hidden his face from me, his face of glory. He has revealed his suffering, humbled face, the man of sorrows who came to sit with us in our loneliness, in our absence from God, in our desolation and wretchedness, in our hunger and thirst. He drank the salt dregs of humanness and has asked me to share it with him.

When I first embarked on the story of my life, I intended to trace its course to the present day but now I feel to do so would be boring and, in fact, unnecessary. I feel that I have said all that needs to be said except for two important developments.

I am sure it will surprise nobody that I faced a crisis of vocation. It was my fortieth year. Up till then, in spite of the many difficulties, I never doubted that I was called to Carmel. Now I began to question not only my own call but Carmel itself. The latter I could more easily deal with. But my own particular way of living Carmel? Was it worth anything? A life of prayer. Where was my prayer? Was I not blinding myself? Was not the continual unhappiness a sign that, in fact, I was in the wrong place? On the other hand, the suffering had gained such intensity that it became a question of 'can I go on, literally, can I go on? I feel I just cannot go on living this way of life any longer. Surely God cannot be asking it of me?' There was the call of the apostolate. 'I was wasting my time. Could I not do more for God in the active life? I would burn myself out quickly and at least have the satisfaction that I had given my all instead of just existing here in Carmel'. So great was the force of this crisis that it nearly ended in my seeking a dispensation from my vows. There was no one, or I felt there was no one, who knew me sufficiently well to be able to assure me that in spite of everything I was truly called to Carmel. Fr Bernard, mistaking the psychology behind the letters I wrote to him at this time, agreed to my leaving. It was concern for the community that prevented me. I saw that I could cause a lot of damage. I became convinced that at any rate, whatever the mistake in the past, it was God's will that I should now stay on. I found peace in this. And this temptation has disappeared completely. I am quite certain that there has been no mistake. Suffering is no sign of being in the wrong place. Yes, God can and does ask us to suffer because this is the way to the fullest happiness. This is the way he opens us up to himself. There is no short cut to holiness, to peace, to freedom, to love.

Very shortly after this crisis was resolved in the way I have described, God succoured me on the emotional level by sending someone to love me, one to whom I could respond from my deepest self. God always sends us what we need and this is especially true of those who have cut off the natural supply lines by their vows. Let them trust God. He will send them all they need. The gifts he gives (I am speaking now of what we might call his positive gifts), though they can be abused, in themselves are never escapes. They come to us in joy and richness, yes, but if we open ourselves to them truly, embrace them as from him, we find that they make still greater demands on us, open up still deeper capacities. So it was with me. This friendship has fulfilled me as a woman in that it has revealed still more my capacities and needs as a woman. What is more, it has destroyed any illusion I might have harboured that I knew how to love selflessly. I have had to begin all over again to learn to love another with a pure, non-possessive love. I realise clearly that for me, this love is the crucible in which my deepest self is to be purified.

This work of 'opening' God carries out in all sorts of ways adapted to the loved being he is dealing with. We can trust him to do it. We have only to accept and this means first of all recognising him at work. I would hope that all I have said may help others to see God at work in the events of their own lives. Not merely the exterior events but in their own hearts, in the difficulties of temperament, in all that seems obstructive, outside his range, positive obstacles to him. It is in this last area that we need to see him most of all for it is in this area especially that he brings us to true poverty.

There is no need to call up all the dreadful things God might ask of us—most cruel sufferings, severe penance...This sort of thing need have nothing to do with the price. The price is a self-emptying which goes on simply, almost imperceptibly, day by day. It means standing in the truth of our being, accepting to be sinners, to feel the weight of our destitution, to experience that we are unprofitable servants and not try to escape from this into that which gives us a sense of importance, success in the spiritual life.

Carmel, as I understand it, is nothing other than the desert where one can be totally exposed to the burning heat of God's love. Even Carmel can be abused; it can become an escape, or rather, in the desert we can look around for little shady arbours under which to hide our nakedness. But the whole life-style is intended to keep us as exposed as is possible in this life, and in this lies our apostolate. In letting ourselves be possessed we hand over creation to God. However this is not the only contemplative way. The Carthusian, for instance, is supported by a vast amount of office, the Benedictine by serious application to study. These are asceticisms; not escapes, but positive means to God; means intended to direct and deepen the contemplative surrender. They again, as everything, can be abused and become escapes. But the very formlessness of Carmel, the absence of supports, makes it a matter of all or nothing. Either God is allowed to come in and take full possession or else there is nothing but a pitiful floundering, a truly 'dead' death. The risks are great, but all the same it is not intended for an élite.

This, it seems to me, is the element of our life on which our attention must be riveted as we work at renewal. How to support and deepen this aloneness, this exposure to God? I am far from suggesting that we must abandon noble, prayerful means of personal development such as intellectual formation, creative work and intimate friendships; rather, these are necessary. To cut ourselves off from maturing processes, to shirk growth under cover of the cliché 'God alone' is, in fact, to escape from God. God is not glorified in half-persons. The more we open ourselves to life, to let the waves of life flow over us, allowing ourselves to feel, to suffer and to wonder, the more we are opening ourselves to God. But always the specific vocation is to be ever more and more surrendered to the Father with Jesus. And is not this the secret appeal of Carmel? Not romance, not mere sentiment, but the often unconscious awareness that Carmel lives out in the flesh what is at the heart of christianity—that 'God may be all in all', or to use another translation, 'that God may be truly and utterly God'. We have nothing to give to God save our complete surrender.

I began this book in the month of Mary and I finish it on the feast of her Assumption. Here is one who believed in God's love, who accepted to be loved and to be placed at the heart of his redeeming plan. Mary assumed, Mary the supremely redeemed one, she is our prototype. And the mortal life of this glorious woman immersed in the Trinity, was lowliness itself. She saw the face of her God in the abasement of his love, she saw him—and gazed on him, her heart in her eyes.

'O holy God, holy Strong One, holy Immortal One!'

'Rise up, my dearest, my dove, my lovely one and come away with me. Winter is over.'

Well, Elsa, this is the end of my book. Do you still think it should be published? Even if not, the writing of it has been a delight to me. My poor, drab, little life! And yet I see it suffused with the radiance of God. Mine is but the common experience, but the common experience understood. If others should read this account of my life, and this applies especially to my fellow religious, I hope they will find encouragement and, recognising the marvellous works of God in their own life, cry out from their hearts with me:

'My God, I thank you for the glory of my life.'